Touch and Go Landings in the 737NGX

Handle your 737 like an expert

Jonathan Fyfe

For Janos and Asher

With special thanks to my wife Kathy for her extra support and input over the months that it took to compile this book - during which time I spent many hours above my usual quota in front of the simulator and word processor!

Contents

GLOSSARY

Term	Definition
A/P	Autopilot
A/T	Autothrottle
AFE	Above Field Elevation
APU	Auxiliary Power Unit
CDU	Control Display Unit
CWS	Control Wheel Steering
DU	Display Unit
F/D	Flight Director
FCOM	Flight Crew Operations Manual
FCTM	Flight Crew Training Manual
FMA	Flight Mode Annunciator
FMC	Flight Management Computer
FPM	Feet Per Minute
FPPM	Flight Planning and Performance Manual
FQI	Fuel Quantity Indicator
FT	Feet
HDG SEL	Heading Select
IAS	Indicated Airspeed
MCP	Mode Control Panel
N1	Low Pressure Rotor Speed
ND	Navigation Display
OAT	Outside Air Temperature
PAPI	Precision Approach Path Indicator
PFD	Primary Flight Display
QRH	Quick Reference Handbook
RA	Radio Altitude
TMD	Thrust Mode Display
TOW	Takeoff Weight
VFR	Visual Flight Rules
Vmcg	Minimum Control Speed (ground)
V1mcg	Minimum allowable decision speed
V/S	Vertical Speed
V1	Takeoff Decision Speed
V2	Takeoff Safety Speed
Vr	Rotation Speed
Vref	Reference Speed
ZFW	Zero Fuel Weight

INTRODUCTION

This book is for users of Flight Simulator X who enjoy realism and have purchased PMDG's 737NGX[1] - and want to learn to handle it expertly in the circuit pattern. The book provides step by step guidance accompanied by instructional images, diagrams and checklists. The setting for the flights is Avalon in Victoria, Australia.

In addition to basic circuit technique, the book covers crosswind, go-around and asymmetric (engine-out) situations as well as rejected takeoffs. Also included are explanations and configuration settings for derated takeoff and assumed temperature thrust reduction. It is written as a practical guide with pre-flight briefs and separate flight instruction sections.

Author's experience

As a real-world pilot I hold a Commercial Pilot License with multi-engine IFR and a Grade 3 Instructor certification and have performed hundreds of touch and go landings in piston-engine singles and twins by day and night in various weathers. I have also had the opportunity to fly dozens of circuits in full-scale 737NG simulators, in both fixed-base and 6-axis motion systems.

Why I wrote this book

The real-world circuit training environment is challenging, busy and satisfying to master no matter what aircraft type you are flying. While learning to operate PMDG's 737NGX in a simulated setting, I became inspired to write an instructional guide on circuit technique for the aircraft that could complement the excellent sector-based tutorials supplied by PMDG. In a similar fashion, this book provides detailed instruction and where appropriate draws upon relevant information contained in the Boeing Flight Crew Training and Flight Crew Operations Manuals as well as the Quick Reference Handbook (QRH).

---

[1] Although written for owners of the PMDG 737NGX, other 737 simulation platforms that have a complete avionics suite and working FMC can in fact be used.

The overall aim of this book *Touch and Go Landings in the 737NGX* is to present the relevant background material and practical instruction in comprehensive detail so as to allow the simulator pilot to gain mastery of the aircraft in the circuit.

In addition to the information pertaining to flying circuits there is material that covers V-speeds and balanced field length concepts as well as a systems overview of the cockpit warning horn logic, control wheel steering (CWS) autopilot mode and the autothrottle (A/T).

If you don't own the 737NGX you should be able to easily follow along using a different 737 platform or to some extent even using the default FSX 737-800.

This is a challenging set of exercises that may require quite a bit of repetition to master. I recommend that you have a minimum 5+ hours familiarization and flight time in the 737NGX prior to undertaking these flight exercises; however, the more hours the better.

You should certainly be able to competently perform circuits in non-jet default aircraft such as the Cessna 172 or Beech Baron. Familiarity with the setup and practices recommended in the official PMDG 737NGX documentation and the tutorials is assumed.

Disclaimer

In addition to drawing upon my own aviation knowledge and flying experience, extensive use of reference material has been made in compiling this book. This includes manufacturer's information, FAA training guidance, and tips and recommendations from other well regarded sources.

Whilst every effort has been made to ensure accuracy and correctness, the techniques discussed and demonstrated in this book, along with any accompanying images, diagrams, charts, navigation data or other operational content should only be applied in an entertainment context and used for simulation purposes.

Some of the concepts outlined are done so at an introductory level to give a general overview and provide perspective for the simulator enthusiast; a bibliography is provided to allow for further reading.

All diagrams and charts have been created by myself for use in this publication. I am not affiliated with PMDG or Boeing. There may be some disparity between the instruction provided and airline training methods.

Software Requirements

In order to fly this set of exercises on a computer simulator you will need a suitable Windows computer with the following installed:

- Microsoft Flight Simulator X (FSX) with SP2 or Acceleration Pack.
- Precision Manuals PMDG 737NGX

Optional

The system used to capture screen shots for this publication also had the following installed.

- Orbx ftx Avalon (YMAV) scenery
- Orbx ftx AU Blue Temperate South scenery

The 737NGX-800WL

737NGX-800WL in the PMDG House livery

Our aircraft for these training sessions is the Boeing 737-800NG which in the real world is powered by two CFM56-7B engines and is one of the most popular and successful airliner variants of all time. Live air traffic websites often show more than 1,200 737s in the air at any one time around the world! PMDG simulations (www.precisionmanuals.com) produce the 737NGX simulation software - under license from Boeing Management Company - that allows us to experience the Boeing 737NG in unprecedented detail within Microsoft Flight Simulator X.

Handling Familiarization

Prior to conducting the circuit training exercises detailed in this book, if you haven't operated the NGX for some time or have a low number of hours on it, I'd suggest taking the aircraft up for some general familiarization flying.

To do this, configure the aircraft as per the Lesson 1 groundwork, then takeoff from Avalon on RWY 36 maintaining runway heading and climb to 3,000 ft. Speed and flap retraction schedule for TOW 48,400 kg is provided below. Use the autothrottle and keep the speed limited to 230 kts.

As a suggestion, perform a rate one 360 degree turn and roll out on the original heading and altitude. Climb and descend 1,000 ft and practice levelling off. Note the pitch attitudes required and keep the rate of descent/ascent to below 1,000 fpm. Perform some steep turns at 45 degrees angle of bank. Now practice flying in the landing configuration, using 130 kts and flaps 30. Perform some 90 degree heading changes in this configuration using 25 degrees angle of bank.

Cleanup and maneuver for a 10 nm final at 190 kts and 3,000 ft, configuring for landing as per the speed and flap extension schedule below. Descend at around 700 fpm. If you are landing from the north on RWY 18 you can set CRS to 176° and tune the ILS to 109.5 for additional guidance.

Flap Schedules and V-speeds for familiarization session

Take off with flaps 5 and land with flaps 30.
V1=118 kts, Vr=118 kts, V2=121 kts, Vref30=127 kts, Vref40=120 kts

Retraction

Setting	Accelerating through speed/bug/alt	Then Action
Flaps 5	150 kts / 1,000 ft[2]	Flaps 1
Flaps 1	Speed bug "1" (170 kts)	Flaps UP

Extension

Slowing through speed/bug	Then Action	Then Set Speed
190 "Up"	Flaps 1	170 (Vref40 +50)
170 "1"	Flaps 5	150 (Vref40 +30)
150 "5"	Gear Down then Flaps 15	140 (Vref40 +20)
140 "15"	Flaps 30	132 (Vref30 + 5)

---

[2] Boeing suggest 1,000 ft AFE for commencing flap retraction during training flights

Lesson 1 – Standard Circuits

Groundwork

Exercise overview

Today's flight will be a "no wind" circuit training exercise with the objective of practicing handling the aircraft in a compact circuit pattern. Although circuit training places emphasis on approach and landing, all legs of the circuit will be examined as they are all critical elements for achieving a satisfactory outcome.

Two circuits will be flown - a touch and go then a full stop. As the airfield is almost at sea level (35'), the altimeter readings can also be used to indicate approximate height above the field elevation (AFE). Be mindful though when using a different airport that this likely will not apply.

Barometrics

In aviation use, altimeters are set to one of three reference datums;

- QNH is the barometric altimeter setting that causes an altimeter to read airfield elevation above mean sea level when on the airfield; this is the setting normally used when below the transition altitude[3].

- QNE is 1,013.25 hPa (29.92 in Hg) - the standard atmosphere barometric altimeter setting used for flight above the transition level.

- QFE is a localized barometric altimeter setting that causes an altimeter to read zero when on the airfield.

QFE, QNH, and QNE refer to radio "Q codes" and are not obscure abbreviations. However some pilots may refer to the mnemonics FE for field elevation and NH for nautical height.

Use of QFE is not widespread around the world; these training sessions use QNH and refer to some heights.

If you really want to remove the 35' discrepancy that is incurred rounding off our circuit heights to altitudes on QNH, use QFE. To do this, when at the holding point, just adjust your barometric setting until the altimeter reads zero. This will be around 29.88/1012.

---

[3] Varies from county to country, end even between different areas within some European countries. However in Australia it is 10,000 ft across the entire country. In the US and Canada it is 18,000 ft nationwide.

Aircraft Configuration

We are going to use the 737-800WL PMDG House variant of the 737 aircraft for our circuit training. The weights are set to kg[4] rather than lbs. (The conversion factor is 2.2 lbs per kg).

The aircraft will be at a very light gross weight, typical for circuit training as it will have a low fuel load and no passengers or cargo. This means that the aircraft will tend to climb and accelerate very rapidly if full power is used. To make things more manageable, reduced power takeoffs will be made.

Fuel Loading

The CDU is used as a de facto fuel loading control panel for the PMDG 737NGX. In real life the fuel loading controls are located behind an access panel near the leading edge of the right wing.

When we board the aircraft for our exercise, 6,900 kg will be entered and 6.9 will show on the Upper Display Unit's Fuel Quantity Indicator (FQI). Note that 7.0 will subsequently show as the fuel on board on the CDU PERF INIT page.

By definition the FQI should show usable fuel and the ZFW should include unusable fuel. The FMC fuel figure shows 0.1 (or 100 kg) additional; many suggest this is a quirk (modelled as per the real aircraft), but it is likely a rounded up allowance for the additional fuel that is already onboard in the system between the tanks and the engines.

Weights

Our payload today will be set via the CDU to 'empty', that is, 0 pax, 0 cargo. This will result in a ZFW of 41,400 kg - and with 7,000 kg fuel on board, a TOW of 48,400 kg.

---

[4]This tutorial uses kg for weights as the setting is Australia where weights are metric.

Performance Management - reduced thrust takeoff philosophy

The engines in a jet aircraft perform a remarkable job, reliably producing thousands of pounds of thrust under a large range of atmospheric conditions for considerably long periods of time. These engines are extremely expensive to purchase and maintain; treating them well and reducing service intervals is of huge economic benefit – not to mention good safety practice.

Engine wear and tear is at its highest during the takeoff phase - the high power settings used for takeoff are associated with elevated temperatures and increased internal pressures.

To counter this to some degree, takeoffs are routinely made at some appropriately reduced thrust level. The simple philosophy behind reduced thrust *or derated* takeoffs is - why increase engine wear and tear by using full engine thrust when it is not required?

When aircraft are operating at low weight or from a long runway, this philosophy can come into play. Takeoff performance tables and charts are consulted to determine the minimum takeoff power that can be used for a given situation.

Derated Engines

Firstly note that engines can be derated to customer specification by the manufacturer as a semi-permanent setting. This is accomplished via an engineering setting in the engine management system as well as changes to other system components - and as such the flight crew cannot make any changes to this configuration. The discussion below however is related to crew-selectable derate, which is used for the takeoff (and optionally the climb) segment.

Takeoff Derate

The engines can be derated for takeoff from the cockpit by selecting TO-1 or TO-2 (takeoff 1 or 2) on the N1 LIMIT page on the CDU. So for example an engine that is flat-rated to 26K can be derated to 24K or 22K. Selecting one of these options reduces the rated thrust output accordingly and causes the FMC to recalculate various speeds such as V1mcg.

In effect this means that for the takeoff segment the engines should be considered limited to this derated value. Under an engine-out condition, manually applying full thrust e.g. 26K on the remaining engine could cause a loss of directional control at low speeds.

Assumed Temperature Method

ATM is another mechanism for reducing available thrust on takeoffs. The explanation is that by design, as ambient temperature increases, the engines reduce their rated output to prevent internal temperature exceedances. This fall-off in output thrust may start to come into play at ambient temperatures above 30°C.

The Takeoff Field Limit charts found in the Flight Planning and Performance Manual can indicate at what maximum assumed temperature a given takeoff can be accomplished when given the parameters of weight, runway length, and density altitude. The engines can then be 'told to assume' that this is the actual temperature, and hence will limit their output accordingly. This setting is also made on the CDU N1 LIMIT page.

Takeoff Field Length

During an aircraft's type-certification process, a comprehensive set of performance metrics are gathered and ultimately provided in chart form for ease of reference. This provides the aircraft operators a practical way to plan flight operations under a nearly infinite set of circumstances. One such set of charts are the takeoff field length charts.

The takeoff field length charts show the relationship between temperature, air density, runway length, aircraft weight, flap setting and engine thrust. The charts are used to determine the runway length required for takeoff for a given weight or looked at another way, the maximum takeoff weight that can be planned for a flight from a particular runway.

A simplified version of one of these charts is provided here.

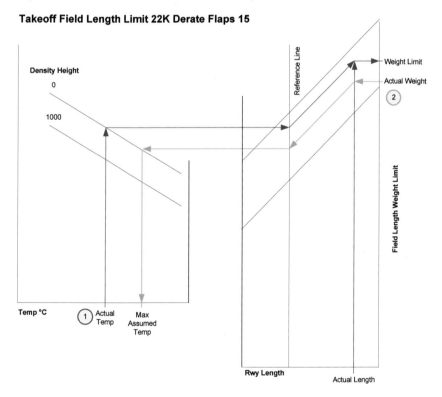

Takeoff Field Length Concept Diagram

ɹighly-simplified example of a type of chart is found in the 737 ɲning and Performance Manual (which is not supplied with the Pᴍᴅ ftware).

To follow the example shown; start at [1] with the actual temp and run a line to intersect with the airport density height line; next, run across to the reference line; from there run parallel to the guidelines to an intersect point with the actual available runway length vertical line. Finally, read across to obtain the maximum takeoff weight for this power and flap setting on this airfield's runway under the current temperature and density conditions.

In practice, a particular flight may need to offload passengers or cargo to reduce an aircraft's weight to this weight limit. This is a scenario that is more likely at an airport that has a short runway and/or is situated at a high elevation, or where ambient temperatures are high.

There is another interesting way to use the chart – to assist with reducing engine wear and tear by planning a reduced thrust takeoff power setting.

To do this, the chart is worked "backwards"; start at point [2] with the aircraft's actual weight. If it is less than the maximum weight for this situation, there is scope to reduce the engine takeoff power required. Essentially, reverse the track across to the actual runway length line then parallel track the guides to the reference line. Now run a line horizontally to the airfield's density height line and at the intersect, drop a vertical line to the temperature. This will give us a figure for the maximum assumed temperature.

Engine Limitations

Engines protect themselves against exceeding temperature and pressure limits; this level of protection changes with ambient temperatures. The trade-off for this protection is thrust reduction.

The concept is illustrated below.

Engine Derate and Assumed Temperature

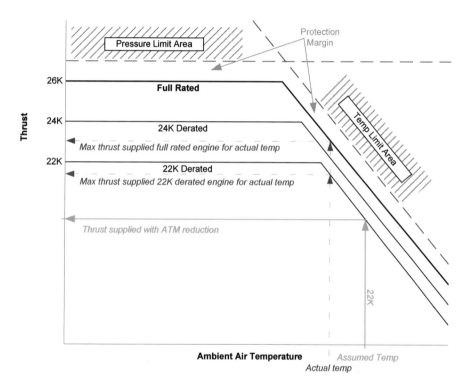

Derate and ATM Concept Diagram

Entering an assumed temperature into the CDU's N1 LIMIT page, based upon takeoff field length analysis, reduces the engines' output thrust.

This reduced thrust setting will meet all performance safety margins, and includes a built-in performance bonus - the cooler conditions that actually exist have a lower density altitude and engine thrust will consequently be higher than allowed for.

Double Derate

As alluded to in the previous diagram, derate and ATM can be used together (if permitted - subject to applicable authorization and company policy) and this is often known as a *Double Derate*. For example, ATM can equally be applied to a 22K engine or a 26K engine that has been takeoff derated to 22K.

For the purposes of this tutorial, we will use the following double derate setting: 22K derate and +60°C ATM[5]

Performance and Speeds

Here are the key values that we will use for our circuit training. These are referenced from the FCOM and the QRH/FMC – for the 737-800 at 48,400 kg, 22K derate and assumed temperature (+60°) thrust reduction.

V-speeds

V1 118, Vr 118, V2 121; Climb out speed V2+20 = 141 kts.

Maneuver speeds

Flap 5 (V_{ref40} + 30) = 150 kts, Flap 15 (V_{ref40} + 20) = 140 kts
Flap 30 = Vref30 = 127 kts.

Approach Speeds (adding 5 kts wind gust allowance)

Vref15 is 133 + 5 kts = 138 kts
Vref30 is 127 +5 kts = 132 kts
Vref40 is 120 +5 kts = 125 kts

Trim

Takeoff trim 3.16 units (with flaps 15 set).
Approach trim - around 5.0 units (with flaps 30 set).

Takeoff thrust

N1 = 85.2%

Flap settings

Flaps 15 for takeoff[6]
Flaps 30 for landing

---

[5] +55°C is often the max assumed temperature used operationally.
[6] For "standard" takeoffs, flaps 5 is routine. For touch and go circuits, flaps 15 minimises the flap travel during the touch and go and also gives a slightly lower V1 speed.

Airport and Chart

The tutorial flights take place at Avalon airport in Victoria, Australia (YMAV). Avalon is used for airline circuit training in the real world. It's a 3,048 m (10,000 ft) runway, oriented north-south and at sea level – ideal for the trainee.

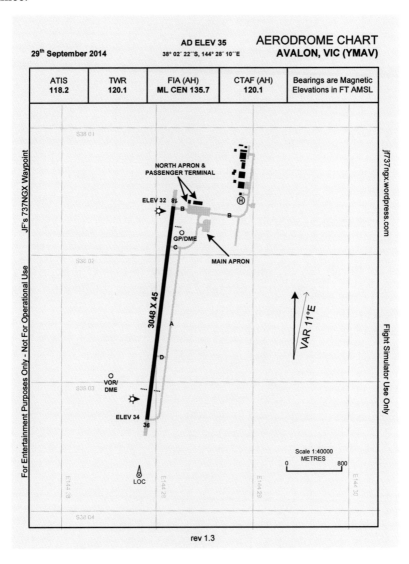

Today we are using Rwy 36 which is aligned 356°M and is equipped with PAPI for visual approach slope guidance.

The Circuit Pattern

Below is a plan view of the standard Touch and Go circuit (pattern) based on the one depicted in the 737 Flight Crew Training Manual (FCTM).

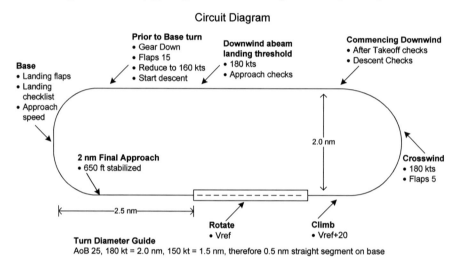

Circuit Diagram

This is an "ideal" circuit, which is challenging to master due to its fairly compact size and the performance capability of the 737 at light gross weights.

Below is a profile view of the approach path.

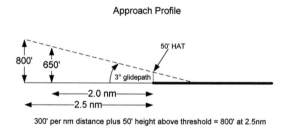

Approach Profile

The threshold should be crossed at a height of 50 ft and the main gear should touch down 1,000 ft along the runway in the touchdown zone, at or near the aiming point.

Runway Markings

Runways have a number of key markings that provide alignment and landing guidance information. The threshold marker "piano keys" denote the start of the landing strip and these are followed by the runway designator number. The designator number is the runway's magnetic heading - rounded to the nearest 10° and with the least significant (right-most) zero digit dropped.

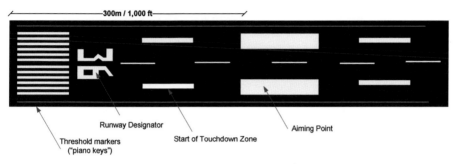

Runway Markings

Aside from the centreline stripes, next is the start of the touchdown zone which consists of repeating sets of rectangular markings set at 500 ft intervals, firstly appearing between the threshold markers and the aiming point bars. They next appear 500 ft after the aiming point bars and may then repeat a number of times, depending on the length of the runway.

The aiming point bars themselves are a pair of large rectangular markings located 1,000 ft from the threshold, between the first and second set of touchdown zone markers. (Crossing the threshold at a gear height of 50 ft whilst maintaining a 3° glidepath and not flaring will result in touchdown occurring after 1,000 ft horizontal travel, coinciding with the aiming point bars).

Consider that crossing the threshold at a height of 100 ft (i.e. just 50 ft too high) will result in touchdown 1,000 ft beyond the aiming point - which is a further 10% of the available runway at Avalon.

For runways with an ILS installation, the aiming point corresponds with the placement of the glideslope antenna; the transmitter installations[7] can be seen to one side of the runway, adjacent to these markings.

---

[7] Often these are small structures or huts painted red and white in a chequered pattern that are linked to a similarly patterned antenna mast

Circuit Area Visual Reference

As circuit training is primarily a VFR activity, it is good airmanship to be familiar with the geography surrounding the airport.

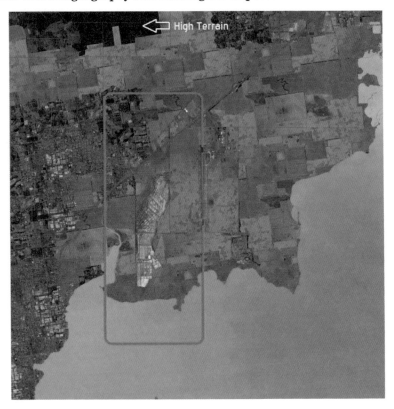

View of the circuit pattern overlaid on the local area[8]

This includes awareness of high terrain, built up areas, water etc. Proximity to other airports and airspace should also be considered.

It can be difficult to avoid hyper-focus on "flying the numbers" but keep in mind that the circuit should be flown with plenty of "eyes outside" time. After some practice you will find the right balance.

To reduce the workload the use of some automatics can be tried in the circuit if desired; the most suitable candidates are Autothrottle (A/T) and Control Wheel Steering (CWS) - you are, after all, flying solo in a 2-crew aircraft!

---

[8] The scenery shown is FTX Pacific Blue and FTX Avalon Airport (YMAV).

Control notes

If you are using a joystick moulded for right hand use, then it can be awkward smoothly reaching for some of the Mode Control Panel automatics such as MCP SPD with the mouse... unless you are adept using the mouse left-handed.

As ambidextrous joysticks are now available on the market I'd recommend acquiring one of these so that you can properly fly as the captain with your left hand - and keep your right hand free for the mouse etc.

Going to the next level - if you have a control yoke you will also be flying with your left hand, leaving your right hand free to operate controls on the MCP via the mouse – it's an even more realistic and immersive option.

To anticipate

The takeoff segment and related activities outlined here will happen fairly quickly, so it is important to be familiar with the expected events and required actions. Our low TOW combined with sea level operation will result in impressive climb performance that can make it hard to stay ahead of the aircraft; the 22K derate and assumed temperature thrust reduction will help to limit the performance to manageable proportions.

To further reduce workload during initial practice, I provide a variation on the standard circuit climb-out, suggesting that runway heading is maintained until circuit height is reached; refer to Upwind Leg Method One in the airwork section for details. This method provides a reduced workload takeoff segment and also creates a longer downwind leg that provides additional time to get comfortable with the aircraft. If this doesn't suit you, just use Upwind Leg Method 2 which follows the standard compact pattern procedure.

First Circuit walkthrough

In this part of the groundwork session, we'll take a look at the planned circuit and the techniques to be used when flying each leg. This will prepare us for the airwork flight lesson.

Takeoff

The takeoff will be a 22K derate takeoff, with assumed temperature method reduced thrust. V2=121 kts is set in the MCP Speed window for takeoff.

The takeoff power is set to 85.2[9] N1.

If the autothrottle is to be used, follow the notes in parenthesis.

Normal takeoff procedure in the 737 is a rolling takeoff; brakes are released, the throttles are firstly set to 40% N1 and both engines are observed to stabilize symmetrically, then the throttles are advanced to takeoff power – 85.2% N1 in this case. (At 40% N1, TO/GA is pressed if using A/T).

Airspeed indication should be monitored and confirmed to come alive. Forward pressure is maintained on the controls until 80 kts to assist with nose wheel steering effectiveness. At 80 knots the elevator input is relaxed to neutral.

> ### Caution!
> *Tail-strike will occur at pitch angles of 10° or more in the 737-800 while the main gear is on the ground*

At Vr, (118kt) rotation should commence smoothly and without delay at medium pace over about 7 seconds to approximately 15° pitch up. (The aircraft should lift off after 4+ seconds at around 7° pitch up). An overly fast rotation rate must be avoided to avoid a tail-strike.

---

[9] FMC values used. FCOM vol1 Assumed Temperature +60° Reduced Thrust (22K Derate) calculates 86.0% N1 (packs off) and 85.2% N1 (packs on).

Initial Climb

Once airborne an initial pitch of 15° should be established and a positive rate of climb confirmed before gear retraction. After liftoff the attitude indicator is the primary pitch reference, but it is important to be familiar with the visual pitch attitude "picture".

Upwind Leg

Method One – extended upwind

I suggest you use this for your initial circuits to gain practice. In this method, upwind is extended until circuit height is attained so as to reduce the number of concurrent tasks; this also has the additional benefit of creating a longer downwind leg that provides extra time for stabilization, spacing, checklists etc. The base turn and approach will be the same with either method.

After the gear retracts pitch is adjusted as required to maintain V2+20 = 141 kts. This will be approximately 15-18° pitch.

Speed Control
If V2+20 has been exceeded, adjust pitch slightly to stop any further speed excursions, but avoid any attempt to reduce it back to V2+20

At 1,000 ft, the pitch attitude should be reduced to around 10° to allow the speed to increase and selection of flaps 5. Note 150 kts is the flaps 5 maneuver speed at our weight.

The level-off needs to be anticipated to avoid overshoot – at around 1,300 ft power is reduced to approx 55% N1 *(or 180 kts is set on the MCP window if using autothrottle)*; pitch is reduced to level off at 1,500 ft at about 170 kts. Power is then managed to allow IAS to stabilize at around 180 kts.

A level turn should then be made to downwind (this is a continuous turn through crosswind, with no square-off).

Method Two – short upwind

Use this method for a tighter circuit once you have mastered the takeoff and crosswind turn segments.

As the gear retracts pitch is adjusted up to maintain V2+20 = 141 kts. Again, this will be approximately 15° pitch.

Crosswind Leg – if you are using Upwind Method Two

At 800 ft, the climbing crosswind turn is started, (you will probably still be over the upwind end of the runway at this point), pitch is reduced down to 10° to allow the speed to increase and whilst accelerating towards 150 kts and passing 1,000 ft, flaps 5 is selected.

Again the level-off needs to be anticipated to avoid overshoot – at around 1,300 ft power is reduced to approx 55% N1 *(or 180 kts is set on the MCP window if using autothrottle)*; continue the turn to downwind, level off at 1,500 ft and adjust power to maintain around 180 kts.

Downwind Leg

An altitude of 1,500 ft is flown and the aircraft trimmed. A track parallel to the landing runway is maintained - approximately 2 nm abeam. N1 is set to around 50% and pitch of around 2.5° for approximately 180 kts. Trim is approximately 5.0 units. When planning a Touch & Go the spoilers and autobrakes are not armed

> *Spoilers and autobrakes are not armed*

Shortly after passing abeam the landing threshold (say 15 sec), the landing gear should be extended and once down, flaps 15 should be selected. (If using autothrottle, the MCP speed should be set without delay to 140 kts to avoid the engines spooling up to compensate for the increased drag). If not using autothrottle the speed will start to decay due to the increased drag without touching the power setting. The descending base turn is commenced as speed reduces towards around 160 kts.

Base Leg

For initial descent, if under manual throttle, speed is controlled with pitch and rate of descent with thrust.

Descent rate to aim for is approximately 600-700 fpm. About 1-2° nose up (between horizon and first mark on the attitude indicator) and 50% N1 should create this profile.

Note the pitch attitude should not be below the horizon at any point – this will result in a speed excursion and create a descent rate in excess of 1,000 fpm.

Base should be squared off for a short time – perhaps 10 seconds. This allows a wings-level assessment of the approach picture.

> *The pitch attitude should never be below the horizon when flying circuits*

Mid-base, landing flaps 30 are extended. Pitch and power are adjusted by small amounts if needed for the approach speed of 132 kts (Vref30 + 5 kts wind correction) and descent rates of around 700 fpm.

Power should be about 50% N1 and pitch should be about 1-2° nose-up. (If using autothrottle, 132 kts is set in the MCP window).

The aircraft should be trimmed.

The turn to final needs to be correctly anticipated; start the turn when just inside 1 nm from the extended centerline. In practice this will occur very quickly, so you will only have a few seconds with wings level on a squared-off base.

Final Approach

The aim is to roll out of the turn on to final on the extended runway centerline around 2+ nm from touchdown, fully configured – that is gear down and flap set, speed and descent stable. (It can be a useful technique to initially aim for the inner left side of the runway so as to avoid overshoot).

The approach speed should be stabilized at 132 kts for our configuration. For the final approach segment, speed should be controlled with thrust and rate of descent with pitch.

> *An altitude of approximately 300 feet for each nm from the runway provides a normal approach profile.*
> *i.e. 650 ft for a 2 nm final allowing for HAT of 50 ft*

If you are on a longer final due to delayed base turn, you may need to set around 55% N1 and a higher pitch attitude initially.

The aim is to stabilize on the selected approach airspeed with an approximate rate of around 700 fpm on the glide path. A go-around should be initiated if not stabilized by 500 ft.

> *Avoid descent rates greater than 1,000 fpm*

At 500 ft, CWS and then the A/T should be disconnected if engaged. Below this height, the landing is primarily visual (eyes outside), with some instrument cross-reference – e.g. airspeed and rate of descent.

Landing

Aim to continue the stable approach and be crossing the threshold at 50 ft. The throttles should be retarded at 30 ft, and a slight flare should be initiated.

The objective is a firm landing in the touchdown zone, not a smooth landing before or after the zone. At low weights, the NGX floats in ground effect very easily, so ensure the pitch adjustment for the flare is very minimal – just adjust by around 2° or so. Touchdown should occur at no less than Vref – 5. Any speed slower than Vref -10 will significantly reduce the aft body clearance and risk a tail-strike.

Flare Notes

Flaring a light propeller driven aircraft involves "holding off" the touchdown while speed dissipates and the descent rate reduces to almost nothing to achieve a smooth landing. In the case of jet aircraft, as the engines continue to produce some thrust at idle power setting, holding the aircraft off during the flare in an attempt to make a smooth landing will result in a greatly increased landing distance. Holding off may also lead to a high nose up attitude and increase the possibility of a tail-strike.

It should take around 5-7 seconds from the time the airplane passes the start of the runway until touchdown and during this time about 5 kts of speed will be "washed off". The flare is initiated in the 737 at 30 ft RA by increasing the pitch attitude just enough to reduce the sink rate to about 200 fpm. Basically the aircraft should really be flown on to the touchdown aiming point with approximately a 4-5° nose up attitude.

After touchdown

Flaps are set to flaps 15 and the trim reset to around 3½ units. The spoilers must be confirmed as remaining down. Maintain centerline track with rudder inputs.

Subsequent Takeoff (Touch and Go)

The thrust levers are moved to approximately 40% N1. (In the real cockpit, placing the throttle levers in the vertical position, also known as "standing them up" provides this power setting, and is a quick way to set initial power whilst the touch and go is in progress).

> *The takeoff configuration warning horn may sound briefly when the thrust levers are advanced if the flaps have not completed retraction to less than flaps 25*

When the engines are stabilized together at 40% N1, takeoff thrust of 85.2% N1 is set. At Vref15 (133 kts) the aircraft should be rotated to approximately 15° pitch for a climb out at Vref+15 = 148 kts.

The previous circuit procedure is then repeated for the subsequent circuit.

To keep in mind...

Although circuit training is primarily used for approach and landing practice, and the emphasis is not on takeoff and climb, you can "feel" a good circuit is underway when:

- you stabilize onto downwind early at target altitude and speed
- you have not exceeded altitude or speed in reaching the above.
- lateral spacing is good
- trim is set and the aircraft can fly hands-off
- there is time to relax and look outside the cockpit on downwind
- you have time to review the descent and approach
- you are mentally "ahead" of the aircraft

Achieving the above will give you the best chance of a stable approach and successful landing...

That's it for our briefing. Following this are some systems notes and then the flight lesson.

Systems – 1

Cockpit Warning Horn notes

The 737 cockpit warning horn is often a source of confusion[10] so it is worth a review. The horn only operates in 3 situations, as follows:

On the ground – when advancing the throttles for takeoff

Intermittent horn - Takeoff Config warning

- trailing edge flaps are not in the 1 to 25 position for take off
- leading edge devices are not configured for take off
- speed brake lever is not in the down position
- spoilers are not down with the speed brake lever in the down position
- parking brake is set
- stabilizer trim is not set in the take off range.

In the air

Intermittent horn - Cabin Pressurization warning

- cabin altitude at 10,000 ft or higher

Steady horn - Landing Config warning (Gear not down & locked)

- flaps <= 10 and below 800 ft RA with thrust levers less than 20°
- flaps 15 through 25 with thrust levers less than 20°
- flaps > 25 and below 800 ft RA with thrust levers less than 20°

---

[10] One famous example was the HELIOS 522 crash on 14th August 2005. The 737-300 aircraft took off with the pressurization control set to MAN instead of AUTO, and during the climb the cabin altitude warning horn eventually sounded - but was mis-identified as a latent takeoff config warning. In the ensuing confusion, with increasing cabin altitude, crew and passengers' consciousness was subsequently lost; the aircraft eventually ran out of fuel and crashed. Although the cabin altitude and takeoff config warnings sound identical, it is not possible for takeoff config to sound once airborne; had the crew known this simple fact the crash could surely have been avoided.

Autopilot notes - Control Wheel Steering (CWS)

CWS is a powerful and very useful autopilot mode that is not discussed very frequently and is often overlooked.

Indeed, in a computer flight simulator where control pressures are absent, CWS can be thought of as "magic trim" function. It's possible that CWS adds even more "value" to a flight simulator than a real aircraft with control pressures, but in any case, it is a flight control mode that can be very satisfying to use.

In a nutshell, CWS will maintain pitch and roll that you have set with the yoke (or joystick) when you release all control pressure.

I highly recommend familiarizing yourself with CWS in the PMDG 737NGX; it's an amazing augmentation to hand flying and will greatly assist you in your circuit training exercises by reducing pilot workload in the busy circuit environment - especially as you are flying as single-pilot!

From FCOM vol 2 (4.10.18) - Notes on CWS:

When control pressure released, A/P holds existing attitude. If aileron pressure released with 6 degrees or less bank, the A/P rolls wings level and holds existing heading.

Heading hold feature inhibited below 1500 feet RA with gear down.

Flap Speeds

The flap maneuvering speed is the recommended operating speed during takeoff or landing operations. These speeds guarantee full maneuver capability of *at least* 40° of bank[11] / 1.3 G's.

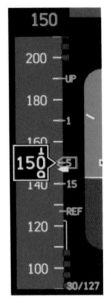

The maneuver speed associated with each flap setting is indicated by green flap setting bugs adjacent to the IAS tape speeds.

Each flap setting also has an associated *minimum* maneuver speed - which is indicated for the current flap setting by the top of the lower amber band on the airspeed display (123 kts illustrated here with flaps 5), and is the speed that guarantees a full maneuver capability of *up to* 40° of bank/1.3 G's. The middle of the amber band provides "adequate" maneuver capability, up to 30° of bank/1.2 G's.

The lower end of the amber band and the first red square indicates stick shaker activation speed – from where a recovery is possible without incurring a stall if pilot response is prompt and correct.

During flap retraction, selection of the next flap position is made when reaching the maneuver speed for the existing flap position. There is an expectation that speed is increasing whilst retracting flaps; at the commencement of each retraction, the aircraft will then be below full maneuver speed for the new setting (but at approximately adequate maneuver speed) for a short period (perhaps 5-10 sec) until full maneuver capability speed is achieved again.

During flap extension, minimal change to thrust is required in level flight to reduce to successive maneuver speeds as each flap setting is made. If using the auto throttle in MCP SPD mode, set the next flap position then adjust the MCP SPD without delay to prevent the engines spooling up to maintain the existing speed as the drag increases.

---

[11] In this context, bank angles have a 15° overshoot built-in. So a 40° guarantee is effectively considered to be a hand-flown 25° bank with a 15° overshoot (error) allowance.

Autothrottle notes - part 1 - overview

This discussion is a brief look at some aspects of autothrottle (A/T) operation most applicable for use in the circuit.

The user interface to the autothrottle components consists of the A/T Arm paddle switch (magnetically held in the Arm position), front panel push button annunciators, throttle lever disconnect buttons and throttle TO/GA buttons.

N1 values (either FMC computed or manually set) govern the autothrottle limits. The A/T can be employed to manage thrust control for all flight phases - take-off, climb, cruise, descent, approach and landing (and go-around). Engaging the A/T is done simply by moving the A/T Arm switch on the MCP to the ARM position where it is latched magnetically. ARM annunciates on the FMA. Once armed, it is available in N1, MCP SPD and FMC SPD modes.

Flight Mode Annunciations (FMAs) displayed on the PFD.

The three annunciation boxes indicate respectively the current A/T, ROLL and PITCH modes that are selected.

Sample FMA indications for A/T, Roll and Pitch modes

FMA Autothrottle (A/T) Modes

The modes that can be displayed in the left-most FMA box are: N1, GA, RETARD, FMC SPD, THR HLD, MCP SPD (all green), ARM (white). Note that the green frame (around "ARM" above) appears when a mode change occurs and remains displayed for 10 seconds as an attention-getter.

A/T mode transitions during takeoff and Climb

The A/T speed mode is available once the take-off phase is completed. This occurs at ALT ACQ.

Takeoff and Go around (TO/GA) are special modes, activated by pressing the TO/GA switches below the throttle handles (or via a configured joystick/yoke button). For takeoff, pushing a TO/GA switch engages the autothrottle in the N1 mode and pitch in TO/GA takeoff mode.

The A/T annunciation changes from ARM to N1 and thrust levers advance to set takeoff thrust.

FMA indications after TO/GA is pressed

FMA display above shows autothrottle mode N1, blank for the roll mode, TO/GA for the pitch mode.

TMD D-TO 2 N1 limit indications after TO/GA is pressed

The A/T commands 85.2% N1 as displayed on the TMD above. At 60 kts the FD pitch bars on the PFD will rise from the -10 position to +15.

Note that the TMD displays the current N1 limit numerically and via a "v" cursor – both in green. The thrust is not always set to this limit however; for example in MCP SPD mode, thrust is set to maintain target speed.

FMA showing THR HLD

At 84 kts THR HLD annunciates on the FMA's A/T box – the thrust lever servos disconnect as a safety mechanism.

After liftoff when sufficient climb rate is acquired the FD pitch bars will adjust for V2 plus 20 knots.

The A/T remains in THR HLD until 800 feet RA and then the A/T annunciation changes from THR HLD to ARM.

FMA showing ARM

With 600 ft to go (i.e. 900 ft) several things happen. The FMA displays change from ARM --- TO/GA to MCP SPD --- ALT ACQ and +20 kts is added to V2 in the MCP SPD target window. If you are holding pitch as per the FD guidance then you will be at V2+20 already.

FMA indications as circuit height is acquired

This is the time to set the MCP SPD window up to 180 kts and make use of A/T SPD mode. MCP SPD can simply be used to manage the desired speed on the circuit legs. You will also be lowering pitch to 10° passing 1,000 ft which will assist with the acceleration; flap retraction can begin.

TMD CLB 2 indications

Also at this time the TMD D-TO 2 changes to CLB 2 on the Thrust Mode Display (TMD). This concludes the Takeoff mode.

Finally, on reaching circuit height, the TMD will show the next N1 limit, for G/A. The value in the MCP SPD window will now determine the power to be set; the G/A limit is not a target until an actual Go Around is initiated.

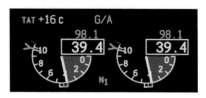

TMD G/A N1 limit indications

MCP SPD Symbols

The over-speed or under-speed limiting symbol appears when commanded speed cannot be reached; i.e. regardless of the setting in the MCP SPD window, the A/T will not command a speed which is less than minimum or maximum speed for the current flap setting. For minimum speed this is approximately 1.3 Vs.

- Flashing A – under-speed limiting symbol

- Flashing 8 – over-speed limiting symbol

Disengagement

Disengaging the A/T is done by moving the A/T Arm switch to OFF or pressing a front panel PB or throttle side button (or configured joystick/yoke button). A/T disengagement is followed by A/T Arm Switch releasing to OFF and the front panel PB flashing red for A/T Disengage.

The A/T is usually disarmed by the crew during final approach unless an autoland is being conducted - in which case the A/T automatically disconnects 2 seconds after touchdown.

Airwork

With the ground briefing and systems review completed let's board our 737NGX for the actual flying exercise.

Start FSX, select "Free Flight"

Free Flight selection screen

Current Aircraft

Select the PMDG 737NGX 800WL House Livery – you can use any livery, but this can introduce differences in the cockpit setup.

Current Location

Select Country: Australia, State: Victoria, Airport: Avalon (YMAV), Starting Position: PARKING 5 -- RAMP GA LARGE, which will put us on the main apron (see diagram on page 23), away from the small passenger terminal.

Current Weather

Select Clear Skies

Current Time and Season

Select 9am, and a date of your choosing; I picked Feb 15 to get the FTX summer textures shown in the accompanying pictures.

Press "**Fly Now**"

Cockpit Preparation

Load the panel state NGX SHORT which has the aircraft running on APU power with the inertial navigation system aligned to S38° 01.7', E144° 28.3'.

Run through the cockpit pre-flight flow and then confirm the key items have been completed using checklist items below.

PREFLIGHT Checklist

Oxygen..Tested, 100%

NAVIGATION transfer and DISPLAY switches....................NORMAL, AUTO

Window heat...On

Pressurization mode selector ....AUTO

Flight instruments...Heading___, Altimeter___

Parking brake ....Set

Engine start levers..CUTOFF

CDU - Configuration of weight in kg

To make this configuration change in the aircraft, go to the CDU FUEL/CTRLS page under PMDG SETUP/AIRCRAFT/DISPLAYS page 9 and select KG under WEIGHT UNITS.

If you prefer to leave the weights as lbs, use the conversion 2.2 lbs per kg.

CDU – Fuel & Payload Setup

Go to the FUEL and PAYLOAD pages on the CDU under FS ACTIONS to specify the payload and usable fuel loaded into the tanks.

Fuel - Set 6,900 kg at LSK1L.

Payload - select Empty at LSK6R.

CDU - Position & Navigation

POS INIT page - Enter YMAV
FIX page - Enter FIX YMAV, RAD/DIS Enter 176/5 nm to assist with orientation and turning final.

CDU – N1 double derate

When referencing the Takeoff Field Limit chart for Dry Runway 22K Derate and flaps 15, for our weight of 48,400 kg and assumed temperature of +60°C, it can be determined that runway length of around 1,800 m or 5,900 ft is required. As we have 3,048 m or 10,000 ft of available runway, this double derate configuration is confirmed as suitable.

The double derate N1 value is configured as per the steps below[12] – note that the N1 limit value is also reflected on the Thrust Mode Display[13]

Setup the double-derate as follows

CDU – PERF INIT

Firstly, select the N1 LIMIT page via LSK6R.

Without any reduction, i.e. 26K, we see that N1 will be set to 98.8%.

The N1 LIMIT page displays the derate options down the left side of the CDU.

---

[12] Double Derate needs to be enabled. Go to the CDU ENGINE page under PMDG SETUP/AIRCRAFT/EQUIPMENT page 4 and select YES under ENGINES DOUBLE DERATE

[13] Your figures may vary slightly. For the purposes of capturing screenshots I had the APU OFF and GND PWR connected. This prevented any fuel burn off and gross weight changes.

Select LSK4L to set 22K derate.

TO-2 Derate - N1 is reduced from 98.8 (26K) to 92.4 using 22K TO-2 Derate.

Now enter 60 into the scratch pad and line select it into LSK1L for SEL (Selected or Assumed Temp).

N1 is further reduced from 92.4 to 86.0 using an assumed temperature of +60°C

The TO-2 ATM +60 N1 limit of 86.0 will be actually be recalculated slightly further downwards after engine start and the air conditioning packs have been brought online.

V-speeds via the CDU and FMC

V-speeds for the flight can calculated by the FMC in response to parameter inputs or be manually set based on manual calculations or other supplied information (e.g. by dispatch). To configure the V-speeds via the CDU and FMC, make the following inputs:

On the RTE page, enter YMAV into the ORIGIN via LSK1L then go to the DEP/ARR page, access DEP at LSK1L and select 36 at LSK2R.

Next go to the PERF INIT page enter ZFW 41,400 (Or use the LSKL3 double-click short cut). This will then calc our gross weight of 48.4.

Add 1 for RESERVES at LSK4L, 50 for COST INDEX at LSK5L and 1500 for CRZ ALT at LSK1R. The EXEC button will now illuminate; press it to activate the entered data.

Now Press N1 Limit (our previous entries will be here); access the TAKEOFF page at LSK6R and enter 15 into FLAPS at LSK1L. The QRH V-speeds should now be listed. (118, 118, 121).

Completed CDU entries showing QRH V-speeds.

Finally press LSK3L twice to load the CG (24.7%) which will calculate a stab trim of 3.16 units. Load the QRH V-speeds[14] by pressing LSK1R, LSK2R, LSK3R.

---

[14] You may have variances of a knot or two. If you wish to, use the keypad to enter in the values 118,118,121 to match the narrative in these lessons.

V-speeds via the Speed Reference Selector

Alternatively, you have the option to set the V-speeds and weight manually using the Speed Reference Selector located on the Center Forward Panel in lieu of a full FMC initialization. You may do this in this instance, using the provided data if preferred.

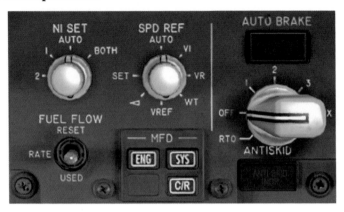

Setting speed reference values with the Speed Reference Selector

When using the SPD REF rotary knob, the selected values can be seen on the lower left of the PFD screens.

→ Set both V1, and Vr to 118 kts.

→ Set Weight to 48,500

→ Vref can only be set when in the air; it should be set to 127

→ Finish up by parking the selector at the SET position.

MCP Setup

The MCP windows should be setup with V2, Heading and Altitude.

MCP configuration

Set the following values in the appropriate MCP windows

- ✈ MCP Speed 121 (V2)
- ✈ HDG 356
- ✈ ALT 1500

Additionally

- ✈ Set COURSE 176 (useful as a downwind heading reminder)
- ✈ Switch on the flight directors
- ✈ Arm the autothrottle

Pressurization Setup

On the overhead panel, F/O's side;

- ✈ Set the FLT ALT to 1500
- ✈ Set the LAND ALT to 0

Pre-start review of today's planned circuits

First Circuit plan review:

- ✈ Extended upwind circuit (climb upwind to circuit height before turning crosswind) to reduce the cockpit workload whilst gaining familiarity with the aircraft
- ✈ Touch and go

Second Circuit plan review:

- ✈ Normal circuit (within 3 nm radius)
- ✈ Full stop

ATC communications

To add another element of realism to the session, you could invoke ATC.

Prior to taxi, contact TWR on 120.1 to request circuits (select the option "remain in the pattern"). You should be instructed to taxi to Runway 36 via taxiway Alpha.

When ready at the holding point you contact TWR again and will be cleared for takeoff.

On mid or late downwind you will be cleared to touch and go.

These ATC steps are omitted from the ongoing instruction, but it's fun to have the TWR communications in play; the choice is yours.

Engine Start

Perform the before start flow and then confirm critical items have been set via the checklist below.

BEFORE START Checklist	
Flight deck door	Closed and locked
Fuel	___ LBS/KGS, PUMPS ON
Passenger signs	___
Windows	Locked
MCP	V2___, HDG___, ALT___
Takeoff speeds	V1___, VR___, V2___
CDU preflight	Completed
Rudder and aileron trim	Free and 0
Taxi and takeoff briefing	Completed
ANTI COLLISION light	ON

✈ Start the engines via the normal start procedure.

✈ Set flaps 15

✈ Set the Trim to 3.16

✈ Complete the pre-taxi flow items. After running through them, confirm via the checklist below.

BEFORE TAXI Checklist	
Generators	On
Probe heat	On
Anti-ice	___
Isolation valve	AUTO
ENGINE START switches	CONT
Recall	Checked
Autobrake	RTO
Engine start levers	IDLE detent
Flight controls	Checked
Ground equipment	Clear

Taxi out

Release the parking brake and taxi out to the holding point for runway 36. You may need a small amount of throttle to get rolling, around 23% N1.

Southbound on taxiway Alpha

It's a fairly long taxi out to runway 36, so take the time to polish your taxiing skills. Pick a point on the glare shield as a reference and keep the centerline running down that.

Cross check by looking from the external spot view. In the real cockpit you keep the centerline running down your inside leg. Also look into the distance for guidance so to avoid having to make constant corrections.

The value of having this down pat is that the technique is also used to track the centerline during takeoff and landing rolls.

Checklist Variation

As the circuit training environment is very busy and it is a repetitive exercise, there are a few after takeoff/descent/approach/landing check items that you may elect to do once, <u>before takeoff</u>, namely:

> Engine bleeds .... On
> Packs .... AUTO
> Pressurization .... LAND ALT___
> Altimeters .... ___
> ENGINE START switches .... CONT

These items can be checked on the taxi and left set for the duration of the session; in subsequent checklists these items are denoted in parentheses to indicate that they have been completed already.

Effect of bleed air on N1

Note that the previously computed N1 limit of 86.0 will have reduced to 85.2 once the air conditioning packs have been brought online after engine start.

TMD showing N1 limit before engine start with packs off

TMD showing revised N1 limit after engine start with packs on

Stop at the holding point

Do the before takeoff checks and review of the takeoff actions.

BEFORE TAKEOFF Checklist	
Flaps ....**15**, Green light	
Stabilizer trim .... **3.16** Units	

Line up

Turn on the following as you move off the holding point on to RWY 36.

- ✈ Landing Lights ON
- ✈ Strobe Lights ON
- ✈ Transponder ON

Terrain note

When on the centerline, stop and view the TERRAIN display. Take note of the high ground (elevation 1,100) to the NNW about 6 nm distant from the airfield. The turn to crosswind should be completed before this hill.

Terrain Display with 3nm range ring

Note the Avalon YMAV fix with 3nm radius and final approach guidance (Radial 176). For the initial circuit with extended upwind we will go outside this reference circle but remain within 5 nm, clear of the terrain.

Initial Takeoff – straight ahead to 1,500

To reduce the cockpit workload, we will continue the upwind leg until levelling off at circuit altitude.

Lined up for takeoff. Note the high terrain 6 nm to the NNW of the field

Do the takeoff...

Remember the normal practice is a rolling takeoff and recall that our planned Vr is 118 kts.

- ✈ Release brakes
- ✈ Advance throttles to 40% N1 and stabilize for 2 sec whilst rolling
- ✈ Advance throttles to 85.2% N1 (Press TO/GA)
- ✈ Rotate at Vr (118 kts) and smoothly pitch towards 15° nose-up (be mindful of potential tail-strike - aim to unstick at around 8° pitch attitude)

Rotation

Smoothly rotate at around 3-5° per second

Passing 7° pitch up on rotation. Note the tail clearance

The same moment of rotation, from the cockpit

After Takeoff

Establish around 15° pitch up with wings level. Look for a positive rate of climb and increasing airspeed.

> ✈   Confirm positive rate..then Gear UP
>
> ✈   Pitch for V2 + 20 = 141 kts

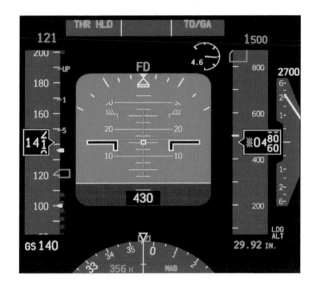

PFD climb out indications

Monitor the attitude, making minor corrections to pitch and heading as needed. Remember, heading can be monitored from the lower part of the PFD as shown above – no need to glance over to the ND.

Upwind Leg

Maintaining climb out speed of V2+20 = 141 kts also requires a pitch attitude of around 15°. Take a visual reference from the outside horizon. Also note that 141 kts is below the flap 5 maneuvering speed which is bugged at 150 kts. If you accelerate above 141 kts, pitch up to check prevent further speed increases but do not decelerate.

Visual horizon pitch reference

↦ Passing 1,000 ft lower pitch to around 10°; as speed increases towards 150 kts select flaps 5 and reduce N1 to around 60% to keep speed below 170-180kts.

↦ At 1,300 ft begin level off to circuit height, reduce power further to 55% N1. (Set 180 in the MCP speed window if using A/T).

↦ Trim the aircraft.

Crosswind Leg

✈ When levelled off at 1,500 ft, make a continuous left turn to downwind – a slight pitch-up will be required to maintain altitude.

Start of Downwind

✈ Maintain 1,500 ft, heading 176°, 170-180 kts - reduce power to approx 50% N1, trim for approx 2.5° pitch attitude

✈ Check spacing – should be 2 nm abeam

✈ Do the After takeoff checklist[15]

AFTER TAKEOFF Checklist
(Engine bleeds... On)
(Packs .... AUTO)
Landing gear...UP and OFF
Flaps...**5**

---

[15] Flaps 5 will be used for the downwind leg

Mid-Downwind

Mid-downwind is an opportunity to assess the situation and make corrections if needed. Trim out any control pressures. Start preparing mentally for the descent and approach.

Looking good on downwind

✈ Do the Approach Brief and Descent checklist

Approach briefing
Vref 127 + 5kts = 132 kts threshold speed at flap 30. Landing will be a touch and go; spoilers and autobrake will not be armed; if approach not stable by 500 ft we will go around.

DESCENT Checklist
(Pressurization ....LAND ALT___)
Recall...Checked
Autobrake..**Do Not Arm**
Landing data ....**Vref 127, Minimums 500**
Approach briefing..Completed

Approach Checklist
(Altimeters ....___)

Late Downwind - abeam landing threshold + 15 secs

- ✈ Lower the landing gear (and set MCP SPD to 140 kts)
- ✈ When down, select flaps 15
- ✈ Autobrake off, do not arm speedbrake
- ✈ Maintain 1,500 ft
- ✈ As speed reduces towards 160 kts, begin the base turn and descent.

Abeam threshold + 15 secs, gear extension followed by selection of flaps 15

Whilst on late downwind, continue in level flight to allow the speed to reduce before turning on to base leg and beginning to descend.

Turning Base - descending

Although descending, nose attitude is always kept above the horizon to avoid speed excursions and excessive descent rates.

25° AoB turning base

Anticipate the rollout onto 086°as we will be squaring off this leg for a few moments. It is very easy during this phase to inadvertently enter a high descent rate. Monitor pitch attitude closely and keep the indicator above the horizon reference.

Base Leg

As per the diagram in the groundwork section, we will fly a short straight section of around 10 seconds on the base leg before turning on to final approach.

Wings level briefly on our base leg

- ✈ Roll out on 086°, looking 700 fpm descent – trim; hold heading for 5-10 seconds
- ✈ Continue to descend at 600-700 fpm using power control, maintaining about 2.5° pitch
- ✈ Select flaps 30 and monitor speed reduction to approach speed of 132 kts (if using A/T set approach speed in the MCP SPD window)
- ✈ Aim to start the turn to final about 1 nm from the centerline at about 1,000 ft.

During the wings-level portion of base, make a visual assessment of the approach picture. Adjust rate of descent or the turn to final accordingly.

Final

When established in the landing configuration, maneuvering to final approach should be at final approach speed of 132 kts. Make small control movements and power adjustments and ensure the approach is stable.

✈ Do the Landing checklist

LANDING Checklist
(ENGINE START switches ....CONT)
Speedbrake...**Do Not Arm**
Landing gear ....Down, green lights
Flaps...**30**, green light

Established on final

✈ Aim for inside left edge of the runway initially to avoid overshooting the centerline

✈ Roll out onto final, heading 356°

✈ The correct profile is 650 ft at 2 nm

✈ Maintain stable profile, 700 fpm descent rate

✈ Power for speed, pitch for rate of descent

✈ Make small control inputs and profile adjustments

✈ 500 ft - decision point (and disarm A/T)

Landing

Well this is the step that brings it all together! A good landing can usually be assured from a steady, stable approach.

Commencing flare for the landing

✈ 30 ft RA Retard throttles

✈ Gently flare by increasing pitch a further 2-3° nose up

Touchdown on the main gear with about 3-5° nose-up attitude

After touchdown

- ✈ Flaps 15
- ✈ Trim to 3.5
- ✈ Stand the throttles up for symmetric stabilization (40% N1) for 2 seconds

It is quite likely that the Takeoff Config Warning Horn will sound briefly whilst the flaps retract through 25° on the way to the 15° position.

Spoilers must not be deployed otherwise the touch and go must become a full stop

Rollout and Takeoff

- ✈ Eyes to the end of the runway, maintain runway alignment
- ✈ Advance throttles to 85.2% N1

Second Takeoff – climb upwind to 800 then turn crosswind

✈ Rotate at Vref15 = 118 kts and smoothly pitch 15° nose-up

Climbing away after the touch and go

2nd Circuit After Takeoff

✈ Confirm positive rate..then Gear UP

✈ Pitch for V2 + 20 = 141 kts

2nd Circuit Upwind Leg

Maintaining climb out speed of V2+20 = 141 kts

✈ When ready at 800 ft, start a continuous (climbing) turn to downwind

2nd Circuit Crosswind Leg

✈ Passing 1,000 lower pitch to around 10°; as speed increases towards 150 kts select flaps 5 and reduce N1 to around 60% to keep speed below 170kts.

✈ Continue the turn

✈ At 1,300 ft begin level off, reduce power to 55% N1. (Re-arm A/T and set MCP SPD to 180 kts)

2nd Circuit Start of Downwind

Note this will be a shorter downwind leg due to the earlier crosswind turn

- ✈ Maintain 1,500 ft, heading 176°, 180 kts
- ✈ Check spacing – should be 2 nm abeam
- ✈ Do the After Takeoff and Descent checklists

AFTER TAKEOFF Checklist
(Engine bleeds .... On)
(Packs .... AUTO)
Landing gear ....UP and OFF
Flaps **5**

Approach briefing
Vref 127 + 5kts = 132 kts threshold speed at flap 30. Landing will be a full stop; if approach not stable by 500 ft we will go around.

DESCENT Checklist
(Pressurization ....LAND ALT___)
Recall ....Checked
Autobrake ....**Arm at 2**
Landing data..**VREF 127, Minimums 500**
Approach briefing..Completed

APPROACH Checklist
(Altimeters .... ___)

Late Downwind - abeam landing threshold + 15 secs

- ✈ Lower the landing gear
- ✈ Select flaps 15 (and set MCP SPD to 140 kts)
- ✈ Maintain 1,500
- ✈ As speed reduces towards to 160 kts, begin the base turn and descent.

Base Leg

- ✈ Roll out on 086deg
- ✈ Descend at 600-700 fpm using power control, maintain about 2.5° pitch

Mid-Base

- ✈ Select flaps 30 and monitor speed reduction (if using A/T set approach speed in the MCP SPD window)
- ✈ Hold square pattern 086°, looking for 140 kts and 700 fpm descent - trim
- ✈ No continuous turn due to reduced speed, hold base heading for approx 5-10 secs
- ✈ Do the Landing checklist.

LANDING Checklist
(ENGINE START switches ....CONT)
Speedbrake ....**Arm**
Landing gear ....Down, green lights
Flaps..**30**, green light

Final

When established in the landing configuration, maneuvering to final approach should be accomplished at final approach speed = 132 kts.

Make small control movements, ensure the approach is stable.

- ✈ Initially aim for inside left edge of the runway
- ✈ Roll out onto final, heading 356°
- ✈ Maintain stable profile, 700 fpm descent rate
- ✈ Pitch for rate of descent
- ✈ Make small control inputs and profile adjustments
- ✈ 500 ft - Landing decision point, disconnect A/T[16] and CWS, monitor airspeed

---

[16] Ensure that your throttle position matches the current power setting by referencing the blue guide marks on the engine N1 display. (Enabled in the aircraft config via the CDU: PMDG SETUP, OPTIONS, SIMULATION page 2/3, SHOW THRUST LEVER POS → YES).

Landing

- ✈ 30 ft RA Retard throttles
- ✈ Gently flare by increasing pitch a further 2° nose up

Spoilers deployed on the full stop landing rollout

Once the weight is on the main gear and the throttles are closed, all spoilers will deploy - and combined with the autobraking, the aircraft will stop fairly quickly. If you wish to use reverse thrust, then this will further shorten the landing rollout. Taxi up to the Charlie exit, then head for the apron.

Taxi back to the apron

Well done – time to head back and review the exercise!

As you taxi in, when clear of the runway switch off the landing lights, strobe lights and transponder, then start the APU and switch off the probe and window heating. Stow the spoilers and retract the flaps. Once parked, shutdown the aircraft and confirm the key items via the checklist.

SHUTDOWN Checklist
Fuel pumps ....Off
Probe heat ....Off
Hydraulic panel ....Set
Flaps ....Up
Engine start levers..CUTOFF
Weather radar ....Off

Need to reduce the pace?

For those with limited experience flying circuits or perhaps low on 737NGX hours - or if the lesson elements just seem difficult to manage in the available time, consider flying an expanded circuit.

For example, doubling the lateral and vertical dimensions will provide an easier transition into becoming familiar with the circuit environment. And rest assured this has good practice value - as it is perfectly normal in real arrival situations[17] to be vectored on to a downwind at 3,000 ft with a 4 nm spacing.

When comfortable with things, revert to the circuit dimensions outlined on the earlier diagram.

---

[17] Arrival planning guide; aim for 10,000 ft AFE, 250 kts at 30 nm out. Reduce to 3,000 ft AFE and flaps up maneuver speed by around 10 nm out – using a descent rate of around 1,200 fpm.

Lesson 2 Missed Approach and Crosswind Circuits

Groundwork

Exercise overview

Today's flight will be another circuit training exercise, this time with the objective of practicing a crosswind takeoff and circuit, a missed approach and a second circuit followed by a crosswind landing with a full stop. The auto throttle will be used.

Aircraft Configuration

These items will remain as per Lesson 1.

Weather

As per previous lesson, but instead of calm wind, 20 kts from 270 will be set. (See the following Airwork section for details).

Drift Angle brief

A wind triangle computation can be used to calculate drift angle. There are also rule of thumb methods that give good approximate values and that is the method adopted here.

Firstly, the so called clock face method can be used to approximate the crosswind and headwind vector components. For wind at 15 off-heading use ¼ for the crosswind component. (15 minutes is a quarter of an hour). For wind at 30 off-heading use ½ for the crosswind component. (30 minutes is a half of an hour). For wind at 45 off-heading use ¾ for the crosswind component. (45 minutes is three quarters of an hour). For greater angles, assume full component[18].

As an example, for wind 310/20 - that is approx 45° off the 356° runway heading. Therefore the crosswind component is approx 20 x ¾ = 15 kts.

In this exercise however with wind set at 270/20 that is approx 90° off-heading so we allow for the full 20 kts component.

Secondly it is necessary to calculate the drift angle so it can be offset to fly the correct track and maintain the circuit pattern spacing. A rule of thumb method is divide the crosswind component by the TAS expressed in nm/min. At circuit height TAS is virtually equivalent to IAS.

Looking at some examples it can be seen to be quite straight forward.

---

[18] The FPPM provides a Wind Component reference chart.

Examples with a 20 kt crosswind component

Downwind IAS 180 kts/60 = 3 nm/min. The drift angle to use on downwind can be approximated as $20 \div 3 \approx 7°$.

Approach IAS 132 kts/60 ≈ 2 nm/min. The drift angle to use on approach can be approximated as $20 \div 2 = 10°$.

Effects of Wind
Intended track 360° with wind from 270°

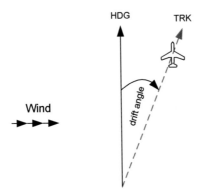

Drift whilst heading on intended track, no allowance for wind

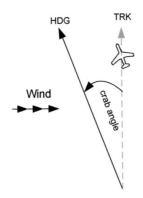

Allow for wind with crab heading to maintain planned track

Effect of wind on heading and track

Heading and Track – Nav Display

Many airline aircraft are configured with Heading Up[19] rather than Track Up on the ND. There are arguments in favour of both configurations, but to me it makes sense that the HDG aligns with the top of the ND which aligns with the actual direction the aircraft is pointing. Even with HDG Up, TRK display is still provided - as can be seen below - and this becomes apparent with a reasonable crosswind and low forward speed such as during approach.

ND configured HDG Up also showing the Track Guide

The above display shows final approach tracking 356° but with a heading of 348° being used to lay off drift. The white track line overlays the extended 176° fix radial.

---

[19] This can be configured via CDU settings – PMDG SETUP / AIRCRAFT / DISPLAYS page 5 "ND"
– TRACK UP → NO

Crosswind Circuit Procedure

The procedure builds upon the foundations set in the previous lesson. Rather than repeat everything, only the essential modifiers are discussed.

Mastery of crosswinds can involve a seat-of-the-pants element that can be pretty hard to emulate satisfactorily in a simulator, but nevertheless the exercise is still very valuable and well worth being familiar with, as more often than not you will have some crosswind component when in the circuit and whilst landing.

Takeoff

In a light aircraft the usual crosswind takeoff technique is to hold the control wheel "into wind" i.e. the windward aileron will be raised and the lee aileron lowered.

In passenger aircraft, roll control is usually augmented with spoilers; these assist with the roll by reducing lift and also create drag that counters adverse yaw. The spoilers will commence deployment with a small degree of aileron input – anything greater than around 10°. It is undesirable to introduce a lift reduction or drag component into the takeoff segment so this procedure needs to be carefully applied.

Spoiler activation with small aileron inputs

The image above shows the flight spoilers starting to deploy even though there is a relatively small aileron movement.

The usual crosswind takeoff technique to use in the 737 is to start with neutral control wheel and maintain direction with rudder. A very small amount of aileron input can be introduced – below the amount required to activate the spoilers; this will assist keeping wings level at rotation.

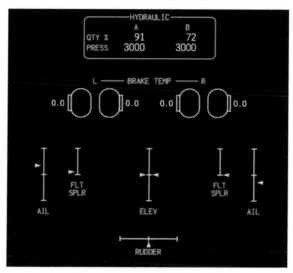

Lower DU Systems Display - Spoiler activation with small aileron inputs

The lower DU when set to SYS mode shows the spoiler movement in response to control-wheel roll inputs.

At lift-off, the rudder input must be removed otherwise the aircraft can roll sharply at a low height – not a desirable outcome. Immediately after liftoff, the aircraft will also have a natural tendency to continue to weathervane a few degrees into the crosswind (mainly in response to removal of rudder input), but you will likely need to increase the offset allowance so as to maintain track. This can be fine-tuned after gear retraction and a climb at V2+20 is established.

Upwind Leg

Heading is adjusted into wind (approx 10°) so as to track the extended centerline, as per the drift angle brief. After the gear is retracted pitch is adjusted as required to maintain V2+20 = 141 kts. As before, this will be approximately 15-18° pitch.

At 1,000 ft, the pitch attitude should be reduced to around 10° to allow the speed to increase and subsequent selection of flaps 5. Tracking of the extended centerline should be verified on the ND and crab angle adjusted if needed.

Once again the level-off needs to be anticipated to avoid overshoot – at around 1,300 ft start to pitch forward for level flight.

Crosswind Leg

Unlike the previous session, in this instance the crosswind leg of the circuit should be squared-off for a short while (e.g. 15 sec or so) as the aircraft will be flying into a 20 kt headwind. This is done to create the 2 nm spacing needed for the downwind leg - and the subsequent turn to final.

Downwind Leg

Downwind is flown normally but with a heading to lay off drift - approx 7° into wind so as to track parallel to the runway and maintain correct spacing. The track and spacing can be monitored on the ND.

Base Leg

A continuous turn should be flown in this instance - don't plan to square off as you have a tailwind on the base leg. Squaring-off base will result in a centerline overshoot.

The turn onto final should be continued through runway heading by an additional 10° in anticipation of the crosswind drift. (If you do rollout onto runway heading and the turn has been too tight, maintain the runway heading and allow crosswind drift to correct the situation before applying a crab angle).

Final

Centerline tracking should be maintained with a crab angle into wind and wings should be level.

Crosswind Landing Techniques

Crosswind approach and landings with a component more than a few knots require careful attention and there are some alternative landing techniques to consider.

Regardless of the chosen landing technique, all approaches are initially established with a crab offset. In the crab approach wings are kept level and slight heading adjustments are made so as to maintain the approach track. Although this is done visually, the ND can be cross-checked to verify if the amount of crab is laying off the drift and the centerline is being tracked accurately.

The methods for performing crosswind landings are:

- ✈ crab/de-crab technique (with removal of crab in flare)
- ✈ crab touchdown technique (wet runway preferable)
- ✈ sideslip technique - align to runway on mid final, use into-wind slip to counter drift

For this tutorial we will use method 1. However methods 2 and 3 are mentioned so they can be practiced if desired.

Limitations

40 kts crosswind component should be regarded as a practicable if not absolute limit for the 737.

Crab/de-crab technique

This is a wings level approach through all segments. The established crab angle is maintained until the flare. During the flare as the throttles are retarded, lee rudder is applied to cancel the crab and point the aircraft straight down the runway. The yaw will induce a secondary effect – roll – and thus into-wind aileron should be applied simultaneously so as to maintain wings-level. The aircraft therefore touches down with crossed controls.

FCTM notes:

Whenever a crab is maintained during a crosswind approach, offset the flight deck on the upwind side of centerline so that the main gear touches down in the center of the runway.

Crab touchdown technique

The crab touchdown involves maintaining the crab throughout the flare and main gear touchdown. Immediate upwind aileron is applied at touchdown to ensure the wings remain level – the into wind wing may have a tendency to lift as the aircraft alignment changes. The aircraft will want to track towards the windward edge of the runway; hence it is important to land on the centerline (or perhaps slightly to the lee side – right in this situation). Due to the misalignment between the wheel rotation plane and the direction of travel, this technique has the potential to be particularly punishing on the landing gear. For this reason, landing in this way on a dry runway where the crosswind is significant is not recommended. The advantage of this technique is that there is no need for a rapid de-crab during the latter stages of the flare.

Sideslip technique

This technique is a transition technique that is used after initially approaching using a crab approach. I've personally found this approach quite pleasing in a light aircraft when things go to plan. The method used is to transition the aircraft using rudder to align with the runway and replacing the crab with a wing down attitude so that the aircraft has a sideways descent component that offsets the drift that would otherwise occur with wings level. However it requires crossed controls and a steady sideslip that can be challenging in the simulator in the absence of realistic control-surface force-feedback. The steady sideslip has to be adjusted to cater for turbulence and gusts. The main gear on the upwind side touches down first and increased inputs to the upwind aileron should be made to ensure the wings remain level when the other gear touches down. Note that this wing-low technique has ground clearance implications and as a guide should not be used for crosswinds exceeding 20 kts at flaps 30.

Missed Approach Procedure

A missed approach can be initiated for several reasons; for example due to poor visibility, a technical problem, conflicting traffic, windshear or perhaps dissatisfaction with the stability of the approach.

To engage Go Around mode, either of the TO/GA buttons below the throttles is pressed; flight director guidance will "come alive". Flaps 15 should then be selected and pitch attitude adjusted to 15° nose up (as per the flight director guidance).

Missed Approach Profile

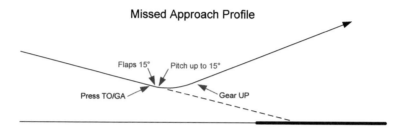

Finally, positive rate of climb should be confirmed.. and Gear Up selected.

After TO/GA is pressed, the FMA will display "GA" in the A/T engaged mode box and TO/GA in the pitch mode box. The TMD will show the power being set to Reduced Go Around power setting. This is about 10% below the G/A N1 limit. (See Systems -2 for further details).

Continuing on, runway tracking should be maintained (refer to the FD guidance) and at 1,000 ft pitch is reduced to 10° to allow acceleration and flap retraction as during the standard climb out procedure.

When above 1,000 ft and accelerating towards 150 kts select flaps 5. Level off at 1,500, and turn crosswind. Complete a new circuit as per previous exercise circuit technique.

From FCTM

> If a missed approach is required following a single autopilot or manual instrument approach, or a visual approach, push either TO/GA switch, call for flaps 15, ensure/set go-around thrust, and rotate smoothly toward 15° pitch attitude. Then follow flight director commands and retract the landing gear after a positive rate of climb is indicated on the altimeter.

Bounced Landing Recovery Procedure

Bounced landings can occur because the rate of descent is too high and/or if thrust is higher than idle. If you land with higher than idle thrust then the spoilers will not deploy and the wing's lift is not quickly dumped, which leaves the aircraft susceptible to becoming airborne again.

Recovery from a bounced landing uses essentially the technique employed for a light aircraft. For a small bounce, just hold or adjust the attitude down slightly. For a moderate bounce, adjust the attitude down slightly as needed and add a small amount of thrust momentarily to avoid a hard re-landing. A high bounce should be remedied via a go-around - as long as the spoilers have not deployed.

Systems – 2

Speed brake / spoilers

The term "speed brake" refers to the cockpit control lever on the pedestal, and this is used to symmetrically deploy spoiler panels on the upper wing surfaces. On each wing there are 6 panels: 4 are flight spoilers (which also deploy on the ground) and 2 are dedicated ground spoilers employed only on the landing roll; these are the inner and outermost panels on each wing.

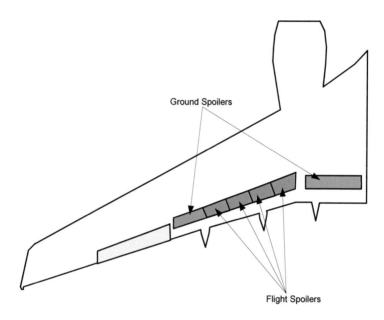

Spoiler Panels

Outside of speed brake usage, the flight spoiler panels also activate non-symmetrically in response to aileron inputs (i.e. in roll mode). Both speed brake and roll modes can operate together whilst in flight.

Autothrottle notes - part 2 – Go Around with TO/GA

As mentioned in part 1, TO/GA stands for Takeoff/Go Around and refers to two autothrottle and pitch modes; this section will examine the Go Around mode.

Typically on a manual approach the FMA will display MCP SPD in the A/T engaged mode box and either blank for pitch and roll mode or perhaps ALT HOLD in the pitch mode box. The TMD will show G/A as the N1 limit, but thrust will be well below the limit, being governed by MCP SPD.

FMA displaying A/T mode MCP SPD and Pitch mode ALT HOLD

Note the green arc on the AoA meter above – this is the Approach Reference Band and it indicates the appropriate range of approach AoA for a Vref+5 approach for flap settings 15, 30, 40.

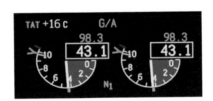

TMD – GA N1 limit but lower thrust commanded by MCP SPD

When Go Around is engaged by pressing one of the TO/GA switches (the GA mode is only available when in-flight below 2,000 ft), the FMA display updates to show the A/T engaged mode GA and pitch mode TO/GA.

FMA displaying A/T mode GA and Pitch mode TO/GA

The TMD continues to display GA but the thrust commanded will increase to Reduced Go Around thrust, which is around 10% below the G/A N1 limit marked by the v cursor. The Reduced Go Around power setting should provide thrust for a 1,000-2,000 fpm rate of climb.

TMD – RGA thrust set

If terrain clearance is doubtful or if rate of climb seems inadequate, once RGA has been set, TO/GA can be pressed a second time to command full go-around thrust[20].

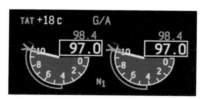

TMD – Full GA Thrust set

The go around maneuver itself is flown manually as previously described[21]. TO/GA mode will terminate when ALT ACQ annunciates and engages (around 900 ft in this case).

If your setup allows, I recommend assigning a spare joystick or yoke button to TO/GA (which maps to key press Ctrl-Shift-A).

This concludes the groundwork for section 2.

---

[20] This however will not be required for our light TOW condition; reduced go-around thrust will be more than adequate.

[21] If a dual autopilot approach is being flown, the autopilot will perform the go around maneuver.

Airwork

Load up the 737NGX from the Free Flight menu and configure payload, fuel, performance and the MCP as per Lesson 1.

Current Weather

For this flight instead of using the "Clear Skies" theme we will customize the weather to setup a crosswind.

On the Weather selection screen, press "Change". "Select User defined weather" and press "Customize..." and then under "Apply weather settings to:" select option "A specific weather station"; it will default to Avalon, Avalon, VIC, Australia. Now press "Advanced weather..." and select the "Wind" tab.

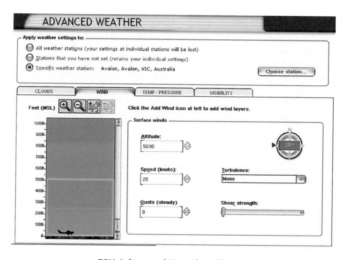

FSX Advanced Weather dialog

In the *Feet (MSL)* area select the range 0-5000 ft. In the *Surface Winds* area set the wind speed to 20 kts and the wind direction to 270°. Leave Gusts set to 0 kts and the turbulence at None.

When done, press "**Fly Now**" on the Free Flight load screen.

In the cockpit

Once the simulation has loaded, complete the Cockpit Preparation, CDU, MCP setups as per Lesson 1.

Pre-start review of today's planned circuits

First Circuit plan review:
- ✈ Crosswind takeoff,
- ✈ Circuit
- ✈ Crab approach
- ✈ Go around

Second Circuit plan review:
- ✈ Climb out from missed approach
- ✈ Circuit
- ✈ Crab approach and full stop landing using crab/de-crab

Engine Start and Taxi

Start-up and taxi out to the holding point as per Lesson 1. Complete the before takeoff checks and the line up actions.

BEFORE TAKEOFF Checklist	
Flaps	**15**, Green light
Stabilizer trim	**3.16** Units

As you move through the holding point for Rwy 36, select:
- ✈ Landing Lights ON
- ✈ Strobe Lights ON
- ✈ Transponder ON

Line up and observe the windsock. It should be indicating a moderate crosswind from the left.

Takeoff – straight ahead to 1,500

We will use the extended upwind procedure for this exercise to provide more time to observe and correct any drift effects. We will also use the A/T for speed control throughout.

✈ When ready, release the brakes, set 40% N1, wait for the engines to stabilize, then set takeoff power via TO/GA.

The aircraft will demonstrate a tendency to weathervane into wind and will drift towards the left hand side of the runway. Use rudder control (and nose wheel steering) to maintain the centerline.

✈ Ease in just a small amount of aileron – just a small control-wheel input so as to avoid spoilers deploying.

✈ Rotate at Vr = 118 kts, remove the rudder input to keep the wings level and pitch for 15° nose up. When you have a positive rate of climb raise the landing gear; setup a crab angle of about 10° into the crosswind - in other words head approx 346°.

Tracking upwind using a crab angle heading to offset drift

✈ Passing 1,000 ft lower pitch to around 10°; set speed to 180 kts on the MCP; as speed approaches 150 kts select flaps 5.

✈ At 1,300 ft begin level off to circuit height.

✈ Trim the aircraft

When stabilized and at flap 5, if you like, use an external view momentarily to observe your upwind track! Adjust your crab angle a few degrees as necessary. Cross-reference your track direction on the ND.

✈   Do the after takeoff checks.

AFTER TAKEOFF Checklist
Landing gear ....UP and OFF
Flaps **5**

Crosswind Leg

Note in this situation, the "crosswind leg" is actually into-wind.

✈   When levelled out at 1,500 and ready, turn crosswind. Hold square at 266° (an 80° turn is required to square-off crosswind as you are already laying off 10°).

✈   As we are now flying into a 20 kt headwind so we should hold this heading wings-level for about 15 secs to give our 2 nm downwind spacing.

Downwind Leg

The wind will now be from our right so in order to lay off the drift we need to adopt a crab angle of around 7° at our downwind speed of 180 kts.

✈   Turn onto the downwind leg and take up a heading of approx 183° to make good our 176° track.

✈   Adjust heading as needed to maintain the circuit tracking. This can be done visually with some additional cross-checking on the ND. Pick a ground feature to aim for.

Demonstrated below is a ground track of 177° with a heading of 183°.

ND downwind showing drift layoff

We're planning a go around on this circuit, so this should be reflected in the approach brief.

> **Approach briefing**
> Vref 127 + 5kts = 132 kts threshold speed at flap 30. On approach we will have a 20 kt crosswind component from the left. A crab approach will be made. Spoilers and autobrake will not be armed; at 300 ft we will go around.

✈ Do the descent checks

> **DESCENT Checklist**
> Recall ....Checked
> Autobrake..**Do Not Arm**
> Landing data...**VREF 127, Minimums 500**
> Approach briefing..Completed

✈ Once again, about 15 seconds past the landing threshold, extend the gear and select 140kts MCP SPD

✈ Set flaps 15

Base Leg and Descent

Due to the crosswind (which on base is acting as a tailwind), the base leg will be flown as a continuous turn on to final with no square-off, otherwise we will likely overshoot the turn.

As a mental picture it should take approximately a one minute to turn 180° at 700 fpm rate of descent to bring us on to final at 800 ft.

- ✈ Start the descending turn.
- ✈ Assess progress half way, when passing through heading of 086°.
- ✈ Set flaps 30 and Vref30+5 approach speed.
- ✈ Continue the turn, use judgement to tighten or ease it so as to rollout on final - continue turning past final to about 345° to lay off drift.

Approach

Crab along final using 8-10° drift offset which give about a 348° heading.

PFD Heading/Track display showing drift layoff on final approach

In addition to the ND's display, the PFD also provides heading and tracking information for quick reference. However, remember that the exercise is largely a visual one with the instruments being used for cross checks.

- ✈ Keep the wings level.
- ✈ Monitor and adjust heading to maintain centerline tracking

With crosswind-only (i.e. no headwind component) the approach is flown as normal with the exception of the offset heading.

As speed reduces, the amount of offset will need to be increased slightly.

Approach whilst maintaining runway tracking

✈   Do the Landing checklist...

LANDING Checklist	
Speedbrake ....**Arm**
Landing gear ....Down, green lights
Flaps..**30**, green light

In a real situation the crosswind may vary in strength and direction and be accompanied by gusts. The autothrottle can respond quickly to this and can be left engaged as per normal. The 5 kts buffer used for the approach speed (Vref30+5) provides adequate gust protection.

Missed Approach

For this exercise, even though you may have a stable approach setup by the 500 ft decision gate, we will perform a late go around.

At 300 ft initiate a missed approach.

- ✈ Press TO/GA
- ✈ Set flaps 15
- ✈ Smoothly pitch to 15° nose up as per the TO/GA mode FD bars
- ✈ Confirm positive rate.. then Gear Up
- ✈ At ALT ACQ set MCP speed to 180 kts
- ✈ Passing 1,000 ft pitch forward to 10° and approaching 150 kts set flaps 5

Upwind

Continue as per a normal upwind leg with a heading offset, prepare to turn crosswind at 1,500 ft as per the previous circuit.

Go around whilst maintaining runway tracking

- ✈ Do the after takeoff checks.

AFTER TAKEOFF Checklist

Landing gear ....UP and OFF
Flaps **5**

Downwind

Complete the circuit as before, however the approach brief is now:

> **Approach briefing**
> Vref 127 + 5kts = 132 kts threshold speed at flap 30. Landing will be a full stop with a 20 kt crosswind component from the left; a crab/decrab approach and landing is planned. If approach not stable by 500 ft we will go around.

> ✈ Do the Descent checks

> **DESCENT Checklist**
> Recall ....Checked
> Autobrake ....**Arm**
> Landing data...**VREF 127, Minimums 500**
> Approach briefing..Completed

Base and Approach

Again, complete these legs of the circuit as before.

> ✈ Do the Landing checklist...

> **LANDING Checklist**
> Speedbrake ....**Arm**
> Landing gear ....Down, green lights
> Flaps...**30**, green light

Landing

The crosswind landing has additional challenges to a no-wind or upwind landing. In real life you are likely to experience strength variations (gusts) and perhaps directional shifts. Our situation has a steady 20 kt wind which should make things easier.

Start of flare and de-crab

With a wind component from the left, in addition to using a crab heading to offset drift, the nose of the aircraft should be left of the centerline.

This will allow the main gear to touchdown in the centre of the runway when the aircraft is de-crabbed. The aircraft will pivot roughly around its center of mass in response to the landing rudder input.

Some into-wind aileron will be needed at the point of de-crab to counter roll; the landing is therefore made with crossed controls.

De-crab with right rudder

At touchdown, maintain track with rudder/nose wheel steering. Use reverse thrust to assist in stopping as normal. The aileron can be centered but some nose wheel steering will be required to counter the tendency of the aircraft to weathervane into wind.

Park and Shutdown

This has been a challenging exercise, quite a step up from the first lesson. Quite a few additional mental processing requirements have been introduced to an already busy exercise.

Returning to parking

As before, when you taxi in and are clear of the runway, switch off the landing lights, strobe lights and transponder, then start the APU and switch off the probe and window heating. Stow the spoilers and retract the flaps. Once parked, shutdown the aircraft and confirm the key items via the checklist.

SHUTDOWN Checklist	
Fuel pumps	Off
Probe heat	Off
Hydraulic panel	Set
Flaps	Up
Engine start levers	CUTOFF
Weather radar	Off

As a suggestion, this exercise can be further practiced with different variations of wind strength and direction. For additional realism and extra challenge, gusts can also be introduced via the Weather dialog screens.

Lesson 3 - Engine Out and Asymmetric

Groundwork

Exercise overview

Today's activity will involve two takeoff attempts; the first will be rejected (RTO) due to a #1 engine cut prior to V1. The stopping point of the aircraft will be observed and brake temperatures noted and monitored.

The second takeoff will involve a pre-set #1 engine cut at V1, and the takeoff will be continued. The position of the aircraft at V2/35 ft will be noted. A right hand circuit will then be flown followed by a full stop landing.

Note that an engine cut at V1 is technically too late to abort; the "event" must occur at least 1 second prior to V1 to allow recognition and the go/no-go decision to be made at or before V1.

Aircraft Configuration

These items will remain as per Lesson 1.

No crosswind component is used for this session.

For the first takeoff attempt, the #1 engine cut will be done by moving the fuel lever from *IDLE* to *CUTOFF*. In order to do this, you may need to perform this particular takeoff with a zoomed-out cockpit view so that you can see the instruments and also be able to quickly access the fuel cutoff and the A/T disconnect.

For the second takeoff attempt, the #1 engine V1 CUT can be pre-set. (See the Airwork section for details).

Balanced Field Length brief

The V1 decision speed displayed on the CDU[22] for a given weight and thrust setting is actually a calculated speed that equates the engine-out "accelerate-go" and "accelerate-stop" takeoff distances. What does this mean? To illustrate, consider a takeoff that is discontinued at some speed, say n kts, and full braking applied in conjunction with spoiler deployment. The aircraft comes to stop at point x. Now consider the same takeoff that is continued. The aircraft rotates and climbs through 35 ft. At this point, the aircraft will be over point y. By adjusting the value of n, points x and y can be made co-incident. The speed achieved at n is the balanced V1.

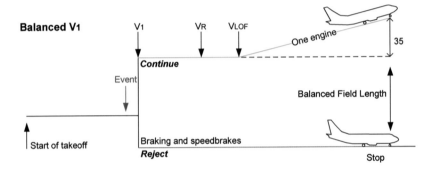

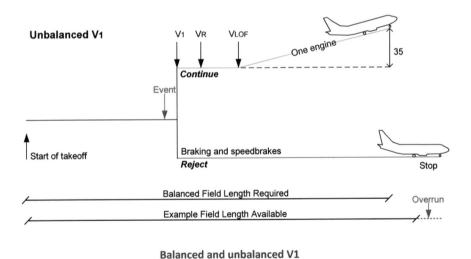

Balanced and unbalanced V1

---

[22] The displayed V-speeds are QRH values; V1 is the balanced V1 speed.

The above really comes into focus when the aircraft is field length limited due to weight. That is not our situation for these training exercises, as the aircraft is at a light gross weight and a long runway is available.

As a final note, for planning purposes, the field length required calculation also takes into account the distance for an all-engines climb to 35 ft with a 15% margin added (i.e. 115% distance). The greater of this result and the balanced field length determines the minimum take off distance required.

Rejected takeoff procedure (accelerate-stop)

The rejected takeoff performance figures are determined during certification and involve discontinuing takeoff at decision speed, V1; throttles are closed, manual braking and spoilers are used.

In a real rejected takeoff situation however, although not used for certification purposes, use of reverse thrust is also recommended to further reduce the stopping distance as much as possible.

For our 737NGX simulation it is recommended to do the following:

1. Autothrottle is disconnected and thrust levers closed. (Regardless of whether or not "THR HLD" is annunciated and the throttle servos are disconnected – this is for consistency of reaction during different points of the takeoff; additionally your aircraft configuration preferences may not allow thrust levers to override the A/T).

2. RTO braking function confirmed; manual braking applied if AUTO BRAKE DISARM annunciates.

3. Speed brakes (i.e. spoilers) deployed.

4. Reverse thrust[23] applied.

The rejected takeoff maneuver should always involve bringing the aircraft to a complete stop[24]. The concern is safety over comfort; the usual smooth handling techniques employed for normal operations do not apply in this situation and the aircraft should be positively "rocked to a stop".

---

[23] Be mindful if the reject is due to an engine failure. Asymmetric reverse thrust could cause directional stability challenges. If this is the case and field limitation is not considered an issue then it may be prudent to avoid the use of reverse thrust. Reverse thrust is not used in the balanced field V1 calculation.

[24] There have been instances where aircraft that were just "slowed" to what seemed a safe pace have subsequently overrun the runway; enough momentum still existed when encountering residual tire rubber in the threshold area that impaired effective braking action.

Asymmetric Takeoff procedure (accelerate-go)

The aircraft's controllability is very good following an engine failure, both on the takeoff run and after liftoff. Nevertheless, positive corrective action must rapidly be applied following the event and identification of the situation.

An engine failure during the takeoff run will cause the aircraft to yaw towards the failed engine and opposite rudder must be applied to maintain direction. This will need to be done regardless of the decision to reject or continue.

During asymmetric flight, turns are made toward the live engine where possible, so as to prevent possible roll excursions. As we have engineered a #1 engine cut, we will use the opportunity to fly a right hand pattern.

Note that minimum control speed in the air (Vmca) is lower than Vr and Vref, so controllability once airborne is initially assured; correct technique is nevertheless required to manage the safe continuation of flight.

Once a positive rate of climb is confirmed the gear should be raised.

During climb out there will be a roll tendency towards the failed engine and the wings should be held level with aileron. Rudder input is used to manage yaw. When stabilized, very little aileron input should be required. Rudder trim can then be used to remove control loads, and should be set so that the control wheel remains approximately level and the wings are approximately level (a slight bank of up to 5° towards the live engine is effective).

Rotation and Liftoff notes

Speed increases rapidly during the takeoff roll. It is common during training for the V-speeds to be exceeded; speed increases several knots during the time it takes to make a call out. Therefore the call to *rotate* needs to be started very slightly before Vr to allow for reaction time. If it is made by the pilot monitoring right at Vr, then after the pilot flying reacts, verifies and rotates, the aircraft may then leave the ground around V2 (or even above V2). This impacts the climb out profile and obstacle clearance margins.

Similarly for calling out V1, it should be timed so that the word *one* is spoken at the V1 speed.

With an engine inoperative, the target pitch attitude is approximately 2° to 3° below the normal all engine pitch attitude; i.e. around 12-13°.

Airwork

Once again load up the 737NGX from the Free Flight menu and configure as per Lesson 1.

Current Weather

For this flight select "Clear Skies"; no crosswind should be setup.

In the cockpit

Complete the Cockpit Preparation, CDU, MCP setups as per Lesson 1.

Pre-start review of today's operations

First takeoff plan review:

+ ✈ Engine #1 manual cut prior to V1
+ ✈ Rejected Takeoff (RTO)

Second takeoff plan review:

+ ✈ V1 Engine #1 programmed cut
+ ✈ Continue with the takeoff
+ ✈ Complete right hand circuit for a full stop landing

Engine Start and Taxi

Start-up and taxi out to the holding point as per Lesson 1 and 2. Complete the before takeoff checks and the line up actions.

BEFORE TAKEOFF Checklist	
Flaps ....**15**, Green light	
Stabilizer trim .... **3.16** Units	

+ ✈ Landing Lights ON
+ ✈ Strobe Lights ON
+ ✈ Transponder ON

Takeoff Briefing

Lined Up for our RTO exercise

So far we haven't been performing a takeoff briefing, so we'll close that procedural gap now. Below is a modified "single pilot" briefing.

- ✈ After TO/GA is pressed, confirm the thrust is set correctly
- ✈ Call 80 kts and monitor all instruments and warning lights on the takeoff roll - call out any discrepancies or malfunctions
- ✈ If any are observed prior to V1 reject the takeoff.
- ✈ In the event of engine failure at or after V1, continue the takeoff roll, call *Rotate* at Vr, rotate and establish V2 to V2 +20 climb speed.
- ✈ Retract gear after a positive rate of climb is confirmed.
- ✈ Set MCP speed to 180 kts and set flaps 5 passing 1,000 ft and approaching 150 kts (if engine-out then additionally set flaps 1 approaching 170 kts)
- ✈ In the event of engine failure identify the inoperative engine, and accomplish the shutdown as per the QRH; then make a circuit towards the live engine side and return for a full stop landing

First Takeoff – V1 reject

Although this exercise is pre-planned, things will still happen very quickly and you will need to instinctively carry out the RTO actions for a successful outcome.

- ✈ When lined up, release the brakes, set 40% N1 then use TO/GA to set takeoff power.

- ✈ At 100 kts, create the engine failure event (accompanied by an imaginary loud "bang"!) by closing the #1 cutoff, and immediately thereafter, at or before V1, reject the takeoff...

- ✈ Disengage A/T and close both throttles; maintain directional control

- ✈ Confirm RTO braking and speed reduction (Use manual braking if needed)

- ✈ Extend the spoilers via the speedbrake

We will not use reverse thrust in this instance.

Stopped after the RTO

- ✈ Bring the aircraft to a stop with manual braking after the auto brake disarms

Brake Temperatures

The brake temperatures can be seen on the lower DU System Display. The indicated temperatures will climb for about 5 minutes after the RTO before reaching peak values.

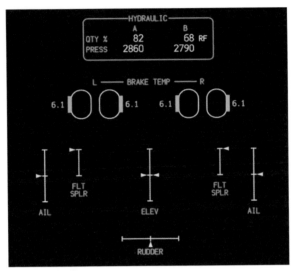

Brake temperatures display on the Lower DU

During a high speed RTO, the brakes absorb a considerable amount of energy. This has the effect of reducing brake effectiveness, and further takeoff attempts need to be postponed until temperatures have cooled[25] to normal levels.

The brake temperatures actually climb for several minutes after the RTO before peaking. To observe this, start the APU and shutdown the #2 engine; monitor the temperature indications every 5 minutes for 30 minutes.

---

[25] The FPPM provides a Recommended Brake Cooling Schedule chart that determines a 30 min wait time based on our weight, reject speed, pressure altitude and OAT.

Engine Re-start and Taxi

After the brakes have cooled for 30 mins as per the schedule (and #1 engine has been repaired!), re-start the engines and perform the standard cockpit pre-flight duties and checks.

✈ Taxi back to RWY 36 holding point.

✈ Arm the #1 V1 cut[26] and run through the takeoff briefing

Note that if you don't wait for the brakes to cool, other than reduced energy absorbing capability for the takeoff, you are likely to get a wheel well fire alarm when the gear is retracted.

Second Takeoff – V1 continue

The initial effect of power loss at V1 is similar to that of a strong crosswind gust. Next, upon continuing the takeoff, you will quickly become aware that the aircraft performance is dramatically reduced by the loss of the #1 engine thrust. However, with proper technique the situation should present no real difficulty. Follow the FD pitch guidance, closely monitor airspeed and ensure a positive rate of climb is established. It should not be necessary to increase thrust on the #2 engine. In absence of FD guidance, you should be looking for around 12° pitch up and V2 to V2+20 kts.

✈ When lined up, set 40% N1 then set takeoff power.

✈ At V1, with the pre-set engine cut, continue the takeoff...

✈ Use right rudder to maintain the centerline

✈ Rotate at Vr and pitch to around 12° nose up

✈ Add rudder and a small amount of aileron input as required to maintain wings level

✈ Confirm positive rate of climb and select Gear.. Up

✈ Set MCP Speed to 180 kts

✈ Accelerate at 1,000 by lowering the nose

✈ Select flaps 5 approaching 150 kts

✈ Level out at 1,500 ft

✈ Select flaps 1 approaching 170 kts

✈ Do the after takeoff checks.

---

[26] CDU ENGINE FAILURES page 4 under PMDG SETUP/AIRCRAFT/FAILURES page 2/ENGINE/PROGRAMMED, select ENG 1 V1 ENG-CUT, ACTIVE→YES

AFTER TAKEOFF Checklist	
Landing gear	UP and OFF
Flaps	**1**

Secure the failed engine

Confirm the engine failure is #1 by checking the Upper DU. Look at N1, N2 rotation, fuel flow, oil pressure and EGT indications.

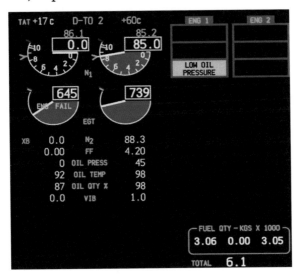

Upper DU showing ENG FAIL indication

Indications here reflect our situation, created shortly after the fuel was cut off. A real power loss event may display different indications, for example a high vibration and/or a low oil quantity, along with reduced N1, N2 rotation speeds.

Once at our circuit height and flying with a greater degree of stability and safety margin, the QRH can be consulted.

QRH excerpt - Engine Failure or Shutdown

```
Autothrottle (if engaged) ..............................................................Disengage
Thrust lever (affected engine) ...................................Confirm then Close
Engine start lever (affected engine) ......................Confirm then CUTOFF
PACK switch (affected side) ............................................................ OFF
APU BLEED air switch ...................................................................... OFF
APU ............................................................................................. START
  When APU is running:
  APU GEN switch (affected side) .....................................................ON
Balance Fuel (Open the cross feed valve)
Plan to Land
Go to the One Engine Inoperative Landing checklist
```

We'll look at the One Engine Inoperative Landing checklist shortly. For now, continue upwind and:

✈   Adjust power on remaining engine to around 65-70%

✈   Monitor speed, looking for ~180 kts

Aircraft Trim

The aircraft is out of directional trim due to the asymmetric thrust condition and is requiring significant rudder input to maintain track. In fact, having the ability to meet this rudder input requirement is the reason that tail-fins on jet transports can appear to be somewhat disproportionately large compared with the rest of the aircraft.

+ ✈ Add right rudder trim, around 2.5 units

Rudder Trim setting

This setting should maintain heading when you have 65-70% N1 set on #2 engine and are in level flight at around 180 kts. It should not be necessary to add aileron trim; the above rudder trim setting should result in a neutral control wheel.

Remaining Circuit – right turn

We will now conduct our return to the airfield via a right hand circuit, that is, with turns towards the live engine. Make a turn crosswind and continue the turn on to downwind; limit bank angle to around 15° and maintain speed at around 180 kts. Trim out pitch loads as usual. We will fly a longer downwind than usual so we can setup for a 5 nm approach at 1,500 ft.

Consider engaging the A/P in HDG SEL and ALT HOLD modes to reduce workload.

Right Turn towards the live engine on to downwind

Once established on downwind we'll refer to the One Engine Inoperative Landing checklist and review the associated go-around procedure.

QRH excerpt - One Engine Inoperative Landing

Plan a flaps 15 Landing
Set Vref15 = 133
Maintain VREF 15 + 5 knots minimum on final approach

QRH excerpt - Go-around Procedure Review

Do the normal go–around procedure except:
Use flaps 1.
Maintain VREF 15 + 5 knots until reaching flap retraction altitude
Accelerate to flaps 1 maneuvering speed before flap retraction.

After reviewing these we can conduct our approach briefing and other checklist items.

Asymmetric Approach and Landing

Essentially normal technique can be used for downwind and base legs. Perform the approach briefing and checklists.

Approach briefing

Vref15 133 + 5kts = 138 kts threshold speed at flap 15. Landing will be a full stop; if approach not stable by 500 ft we will go around using flaps 1.

DESCENT Checklist

Recall	Checked
Autobrake	**Arm**
Landing data	**VREF 15 (133 kts), Minimums 500**
Approach briefing	Completed

Deferred Item

GROUND PROXIMITY FLAP INHIBIT switch .... FLAP INHIBIT

Continue the long downwind leg, turn base and maintain circuit height. Set flaps 5 and allow the speed to reduce towards 150 kts. Select Gear Down on base and then flaps 15. Turn on to final approach, start the descent – looking for 138 kts, unwind the rudder trim and take up the load on the pedals.

> ✈ Do the Landing checklist...

LANDING Checklist

ENGINE START switches	**No.1 OFF, No.2 CONT**
Speedbrake	**Arm**
Landing gear	Down, green lights
Flaps	**15**, green light

During the flare, as throttles are retarded to idle, remove the rudder input – the aircraft will behave as per a normal landing.

Be cautious with the asymmetric reverse thrust.

Park and Shutdown

One engine taxi will be required to vacate. This should present no real issue but remember you will be exiting to the right with no left engine thrust so keep the speed to 10 knots or above. Operators often use single engine taxi (after vacating the runway) to conserve fuel.

Shutdown on the ramp

Taxi back to the apron, perform the usual post flight activities and shutdown.

This last exercise has a high workload and will likely require some repetition and practice for you to become proficient at it. It can be quite unsettling even in the simulator when a routine takeoff performed many times becomes critical due to a failure! It's a rewarding exercise to master and worthwhile practicing from time to time.

Challenge exercise!

This V1 cut exercise just covered requires some practice to master – but even so, there are no distracting fire bells going off and the weather is fine. For an extra challenge, repeat the exercise but instead of a V1 cut, program an engine fire[27] 30 seconds into the takeoff. Set the weather and visibility to poor conditions and consider a combining these settings with night takeoff to increase the workload!

---

[27] CDU ENGINE FAILURES page 4 under PMDG SETUP/AIRCRAFT/FAILURES
page 2/FIRE/PROGRAMMED, select ENG 1 FIRE, ARMED→YES

Review of Balance Field

Comparison of aircraft positions after performing a single engine V1 reject and a single engine continued takeoff to 35'.

Author's balanced field test results

The practical testing for the two scenarios matched with almost the same distance used. The distance was around 4,580 ft for both scenarios. The performance charts show around 5,800 ft required for an actual +60°C situation, but because ambient temps are actually 15°C we see a performance benefit, even with the double derate takeoff power setting.

Summary

This comprehensive guide provides a detailed insight into the key elements, considerations and activities that are a part of flying airliner circuits.

If you have worked through each lesson, perhaps more than once, you will have acquired a new level of knowledge and gained valuable practical experience.

I certainly hope that you have enjoyed this set of hands-on exercises and can take to the simulated skies more confidently and ready to fly some visual patterns under various conditions.

Good having you aboard captain, and happy circuit flying.

Appendix

737-800 Specification Summary[28]

Engines	CFMI CFM56-7 rated at 27,300 lb
Maximum Fuel Capacity	45,795 lb / 26,020 L / 20,800 kg
Maximum Takeoff Weight	174,200 lb / 79,010 kg
Maximum Range	3,115 nm / 5,765 km
Wing Span With Winglets	117 ft 5 in / 35.8 m
Overall Length	129 ft 6 in / 39.5 m
Tail Height	41 ft 2 in / 12.5 m

737 Production Numbers[29]

737 "classics"
-100 -200 -300 -400 -500 & T43As   3,132

737 NG's
-600 -700 -800 -900 & BBJs   5,218

---

[28] From Boeing
[29] From Boeing

The Author's 737NGX flying

The 737-800 is a marvellous aircraft to fly, and after quite some time gaining experience with it, I started taking in interest in the other NG models. Since then, for the most part, I usually fly the 737-600 variant of the NGX.

The flight characteristics of the -600 are slightly more nimble than those of the -800, making the aircraft a real pleasure to hand-fly; after a few flights I became really taken with it, and the -600 unexpectedly became my aircraft of choice. This aircraft variant is available as part of PMDG's 737NGX expansion pack which delivers both the -700 and -600 models.

The -600 is a shorter version than the -800 by 27 ft. The wingspan (non-winglet) and fuel carrying capacity are the same. The winglets on the -800 add 5 ft to the wingspan.

Author's 737-600 Gallery

Janet at Beale Air Force Base

Far away from the training airfield at Avalon in Australia are the skies above Nevada and California, USA, and this is where I usually fly my 737-600NGX, hopping around on short sectors between Creech AFB, Tonopah Test Range, China Lake NAWS, Beale AFB, Victorville, Point Mugu NAS, Mojave Air and Space Port, Groom Lake, Las Vegas, Beale AFB, Miramar NAS, Plant 42 and Edwards AFB.

Appendix

Universal Exports pushing back at China Lake

Aerial view of Edwards Air Force Base

Universal Exports arriving at Phoenix Sky Harbor

Janets gathering at Groom Lake after sunrise

Universal Exports on the ramp at Mojave Air and Space Port

Janet arrival at Groom Lake

Janet exits 32R at Groom Lake

Janet enroute to Creech Air Force Base (Indian Springs)

Appendix

Universal Exports sunrise over Nevada

Universal Exports flaring to land at Victorville

References

Bibliography

Brady, C. (2013). The Boeing 737 Technical Guide. Tech Pilot Services Ltd.

Federal Aviation Administration. (2004). Airplane Flying Handbook. United States Department of Transportation.

Federal Aviation Administration. (2008). Pilot's Handbook of Aeronautical Knowledge. United States Department of Transportation.

Federal Aviation Administration. (1993). Takeoff Safety Training Aid. Washington D.C.: United States Department of Transportation.

The Boeing Company, Seattle, Washington, United States of America.

> 737 Flight Crew Operations Manual.
> 737 Flight Crew Training Manual.
> 737 Flight Planning and Performance Manual.
> 737 Quick Reference Handbook.

Websites

The following websites contain a wealth of useful information and were invaluable resources for my research.

smartcockpit.com
skybrary.aero
b737.org.uk
flyaoamedia.com
flaps2approach.com
boeing.com
pprune.org

Software and systems used in creating this book

Microsoft's Flight Simulator X and PMDG's 737NGX

Each time I load these pieces of software I am amazed and inspired by what I see, hear and experience. I'd like to extend my heartfelt thanks to the talented people behind these products for their incredible efforts in bringing them to fruition. They provide me with many hours of immersive enjoyment.

I hope this book can pay tribute in a small way.

Add-ons used for enhancing the platform

In addition to the core simulation software, the following are installed on the author's system and greatly enhance the simulation environment.

- EZdok Camera Addon (EZCA)
- Orbx FTX (Full Terrain) Australia and Avalon Airport scenery
- Ultimate Traffic 2
- GSX Ground Services

Computer System

A DELL XPS-17, 8 GB RAM, I7 4-core 2.2 GHz laptop running Win 7 64 bit was used for the simulation platform.

The book was written using MS-Word 97 running on the DELL XPS 17 and also on a DELL Latitude E7240 Ultrabook. Diagrams were created using MS-Visio 2007.

737NG simulators

Thanks to the teams at VS Jet and Flight Experience for providing me with many hours of expert instruction in their 737NG simulators. These simulators provide an unparalleled simulation experience and after each session, I always keenly look forward to my next one.

About the Author

An enthusiastic fan of flight simulation for many years and also a holder of an Australian commercial pilot license, Jonathan Fyfe is trained in aerobatics, is multi-engine IFR rated and is also qualified as a flight instructor.

In addition to enjoying numerous hours in full-size 737NG simulators, he has logged over 250 hrs PMDG 737NGX time.

Jonathan has a bachelor's degree in computer science and lives in Sydney, Australia with his wife Kathy and their two sons.

He operates the website **JF's 737NGX Waypoint** which can be accessed at:

jf737ngx.wordpress.com

Other titles by the Author

Introductory Flight for Aerosoft's Twin Otter Extended.

The Aerosoft Twin Otter Extended is a comprehensive and immersive add-on aircraft for Flight Simulator X. It's a fascinating aircraft that is a lot of fun to learn about and fly. It is unlike the 737 in almost every way and provides the simulator enthusiast with a completely different set of systems, engines and handling requirements.

The supplied software package lacks an introductory tutorial flight so it can be difficult to know how to begin properly with this bird - and that's where this instructional guide fits in.

The Tutorial

This enjoyable exercise provides the Twin Otter enthusiast with handling information, speeds, rpm and power settings etc., as well as demonstrating a short sector flight – it's designed so to seem like you have an instructor on board.

The flight takes place in Washington State, USA, and involves a 42 nm (approx 25 min) flight from Olympia Regional (KOLM) to Bannerman (KHQM) - via Elma (K4W8/4W8) - which is located at the trip mid-point.

The direct legs are: 255° for 21 nm (113.4 OLM VORTAC) to overhead Elma, then 247° for 21 nm to Bannerman.

It's an enjoyable VFR exercise, and the route has navaids that can be tuned allowing some use of the autopilot (AP) for familiarization purposes.

This tutorial will give you the confidence and know-how that you need to have so that you can sit in the captain's seat and get the best value out of your Twin Otter purchase!

Logbook

Date	A/C	Lesson and Remarks	Hrs
		Sub Total	

Logbook

Date	A/C	Lesson and Remarks	Hrs
		Sub Total	

Index

Printed in Great Britain
by Amazon